Building Reading Comprehension

Grades 5-6

by
Norm Sneller

Published by Instructional Fair
an imprint of
Frank Schaffer Publications®

Instructional Fair

Author: Norm Sneller
Cover Artist: Matthew Van Zomeren
Interior Artist: Clinton Johnston

Frank Schaffer Publications®

Instructional Fair is an imprint of Frank Schaffer Publications.

Send all inquiries to:
Frank Schaffer Publications
3195 Wilson Drive NW
Grand Rapids, Michigan 49534

Building Reading Comprehension—grades 5–6

ISBN: 1-56822-914-3

8 9 10 PAT 08 07

Table of Contents

Little My Wants

Read the paragraphs and answer the questions that follow.

1 My children are hungry and need food.

2 When my husband was taken away by the police six years ago, we were thrown out of our house. I feared for our lives. But our community enfolded us. Mama helped with meals when she could. My children, Theresa and Angelo, and I moved into the home of my sister. Friends from our mountain community gathered clothes and supplies for us. The padre was a dear, too. He called on the police many many times to gather news of my husband. After six weeks of his pestering, the police told him to call no more. My husband was moved to another province to work on a road project. We have received five of his letters. We have not heard from him these past two years.

3 My sister and I try to remain cheerful sharing one house. It's not easy. She has a husband and four children of her own. So my children and I share a bedroom. We eat with the family, but we must be careful not to take food from my sister's family. Daniel, my sister's husband, tries hard not to complain when Teresa or Angelo leave toys or school books out. But I know he'd prefer that we find another home.

4 I find work in the community. I serve as a maid for a family of gringos living on our mountain this year. I walk to their home every morning, Monday to Friday. I clean their house, wash their dishes, and look after their house while they are gone to work. Because I stay in the home while the family is gone, thieves do not bother them. The norteamericanos are very kind. And their little girl, Melissa, is a bright-eyed love. But I am a maid. So I am paid maid's wages. And money is dear.

5 Last month Teresa needed a new uniform. Because she is now in grade 7, she attends a new school. Her old school's uniform cannot be used. Nor her shoes. So I could not send her to school until we could afford to buy new clothing. So I begged. I do not like to beg for help, but what could I do? I went to my gringa lady and poured out my heart. She had me sit down with her, and we cried together. She gave me money for the purchases and said I should think of it as a present.

6 That was kind.

7 But I do not wish to depend on others' gifts. I don't want charity. Oh, if I could provide for my children and myself without outside help! I see the looks people give us. They stare at our mended blouses and shirts. They smirk as they glance at our shoes that don't quite fit our feet. I wash our clothes by hand and Theresa has learned to do so as well. But we have only two or three changes of clothing.

8 In the season of Navidad, my norteamericana familia gave Theresa and Angelo toys and clothes. They gave me a new blouse and a basket of food. Fruits and rice and beans and sweets. They drove to my home to deliver the gifts. How wonderful to have such a surprise! I showed them our tree of the Christ Child with its village scenes set in place beneath the boughs. But why can I not respond with a gift?

9 My Mama is old. She can no longer serve a family as their maid. She works for the church, but there are no wages for that. I wonder if she can stay here with us. And now my gringo family is returning to the United States. They do not require my help. And so I have no work. Who will hire me? All the rich families have their own maids, gardeners, and drivers. Must I beg? I will not!

10 But how will I feed my children? They are hungry and need food.

A. Write the paragraph number. In which paragraph does the writer most clearly express

_____ her daughter's needs?

_____ how others see her family?

_____ the loss of her husband?

_____ her present fears?

_____ sharing a home with her sister?

_____ receiving gifts?

B. What are the writer's greatest concerns? Rate the following, 1 being the most and 7 the least.
_____ food   _____ money   _____ work   _____ husband
_____ clothes   _____ children   _____ pride

Give your reasons for this rating order._____

_____

C. Should the North American family share some of the blame for this woman's difficulties? Explain. _____

_____

D. Do you think this woman would have the same fears and hardships if she lived in the United States or in Canada? Explain.

_____

In the Cupboard

In 1980 Lynne Reid Banks wrote the first in a series of adventure books, *The Indian in the Cupboard.* Decipher the phonetically spelled words in the sentences below.

1. The story's /**aw´ thur**/ has a great imagination. _____

2. She writes of a young boy learning to be /**re spon´ si b*l**/. _____

3. Omri has a large collection of plastic /**fig´ yurz**/. _____

4. The magic begins when Omri turns a /**spesh´ *l**/ key in the cupboard door's lock. _____

5. Little Bear is an /**ir´ ō kwoi**/ brave from the distant past. _____

6. The Indian constructs a longhouse from /**na´ cher *l**/ materials that Omri gathered. _____

7. Patrick, Omri's pal, at first does not /**be lēv´**/ in the Indian. _____

8. Patrick brings to life a /**frīt´ *nd**/ cowboy and his panicking horse. _____

9. At one point, this cowboy must be treated by a wartime /**sōl´ jer**/ named Tommy. _____

10. The small beings from the past /**jer´ nē**/ to school in Omri's pocket. _____

11. Even a pet rodent /**kon trib´ yūts**/ to this book's adventure. _____

12. Omri discovers how difficult it is to keep /**ev´ rē wun**/ at peace. _____

Fill in the blanks below with the coded letters from the answers you gave. For example, 3-4 means answer 3, 4th letter.

1-4	5-7	3-7	6-3	5-3	10-4	9-5	11-1	1-1	7-3

3-1	6-6	10-5	8-6	4-6	2-3	12-5

note: the symbol * denotes the schwa sound

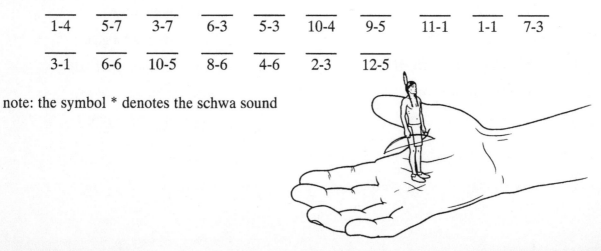

Can You Tell a Book by Its Cover?

Directions: Match each book title with its genre or description by writing the letter in the blank.

_____ 1. *Cousin Clara's Creative Cuisine*   a. atlas

_____ 2. *The Case of the Ancient Aardvark*   b. myth

_____ 3. *Love Me Tender*   c. gardening

_____ 4. *How the Nose Got Its Sniffles*   d. engine repair

_____ 5. *Time to Rhyme (or Not)*   e. song book

_____ 6. *A Volume of Verbosity*   f. romance

_____ 7. *Where Am I?*   g. autobiography

_____ 8. *Mama's Walk to Kyoto*   h. sports stars

_____ 9. *Mein Hund Ist Gesund*   i. East Asian folktale

_____ 10. *Music to My Ears*   j. cooking

_____ 11. *Where are the Clones?*   k. American dance

_____ 12. *Brandin', Punchin', Eatin' Dust*   l. inventions

_____ 13. *Like a Diamond*   m. nursery rhymes

_____ 14. *Hey, Diddle!*   n. science fiction

_____ 15. *Tut Tut, Tut!*   o. mystery

_____ 16. *A Knight to Remember*   p. poetry

_____ 17. *Eureka! It's a Hoover!*   q. thesaurus

_____ 18. *Give 'er Some Gas*   r. medieval history

_____ 19. *Faces for Wheaties*   s. American history

_____ 20. *Easel Down the Road*   t. ESP

_____ 21. *In Other Words*   u. dictionary

_____ 22. *Compost Is Your Friend*   v. foreign language

_____ 23. *If You Could Read My Mind*   w. art appreciation

_____ 24. *Shake, Rattle, and Roll*   x. stars

_____ 25. *I Am What I Am*   y. Ancient Egypt

Moody Blues

Directions: In each set of problems below, match the adjective to the quotation by writing the letter in the blank.

_____ 1. hot-tempered

_____ 2. embarrassed

_____ 3. confused

_____ 4. tired

_____ 5. sneaky

a. "Where are we? I thought this was . . . no, I guess not!" stuttered Stan.

b. "I don't think I can walk another step," sighed Sanders, falling into a nearby recliner.

c. Stomping his feet, Sean shrieked, "You can't make me finish my work!"

d. "Shh! Get your head down, Sarah. Don't let Mrs. Lions see us," whispered Wanda.

e. "Oops! I'm sorry. I thought you were my brother," moaned Martha as she wiped ketchup off the waiter's white shirt.

_____ 6. clumsy

_____ 7. ecstatic

_____ 8. accusatory

_____ 9. foolish

_____ 10. melancholy

f. "Uhhh. Four . . . no, seven . . . Uhh. Is this true or false, Miss Jacobs?" inquired Isaac.

g. "No, just go ahead to the movie without me. I think I'll just stay home and cry myself to sleep," croaked Craig.

h. "Oh, how wonderful! My very own Darby DeLight Dollhouse!" squealed Skeeter.

i. "Hey, I just stepped on your feet, didn't I, Terri? Oops! I did it again!" giggled Garth.

j. "Aww, come on, Ron! You must have eaten that blueberry pie. You've got crumbs on your chin and a bluish stain on your T-shirt," observed Oscar.

_____ 11. obnoxious

_____ 12. spendthrift

_____ 13. timid

_____ 14. effervescent

_____ 15. crabby

k. "Leave me alone! Just get out of my face!" shouted Sheri.

l. "Hey, there's another penny! That makes 42 cents I saved up this week," muttered Mindy.

m. "Ms. Chairman. Members of the Board. Cousin Carin. Thank you for choosing me to be the teenage Minty Fresh spokesperson," gushed Gladys.

n. "What a dump! Hey, string bean! Get over here and take my order," demanded Damien.

o. "Say, uh, Troy, may I ride, uh, with you? I mean, if it's no bother?" asked Anders.

Spinnin' Wheels

Theodore ThighMeister, the top-seeded cyclist for the Pan American squad, has a busy morning schedule. After all, he is a student, an athlete, and a celebrity.

6:30   Walk Hercules (the dog)
6:50   Bring Hercules to pup-sitter
7:00   Breakfast with champions at the
            All-Flakes Bowl Inn
7:30   Take taxi to arena; change clothes
            in private suite
7:50   Stretching exercises
8:00   Private bike practice with
            Lee Schwinn
9:00   Tape interview with Corrie Katik
            from the *Yesterday Show*
9:45   Take taxi to university; have power
            snack (Tootsie Rolls)
10:00   Private instruction for
            Anthropology 312 (bring toothbrush)
11:00   Meet with study group at University
            Library. Topic: caterpillar diseases
12:20   Call agent

Directions: Using the schedule information, answer the following questions.

1. Who interviews Theo? _____

2. What is Theo's power snack? _____

3. What is the total amount of time Theo is scheduled to spend on his studies? _____

4. Who is Hercules? _____

5. What will Theo's study group discuss? _____

6. Where is breakfast? _____

7. How much time is scheduled for the interview? _____

8. Where must Theo bring his toothbrush? _____

9. How much time is spent on stretching exercises? _____

10. If Theo speaks with his agent for 17 minutes, what time is it when he gets off the phone?

_____

Extra: On the back of this page, create a hectic afternoon schedule to complete Theo's day.

Just Friends

"Awww. No!"

Jake kicked at a clump of weeds along the sidewalk outside King Middle School. Yeah, he missed the after-school bus. Again! Man! What was wrong with him anyway?

Now, what to do? Can't call home. Mom's at the office. Dad's away somewhere on business. Milwaukee maybe. And no way could he call his older sister Micah at her school. She'd still be in class. Sure. But, ooh! You don't mess with Micah! She would have a hissy fit!

No. It'd be better just to cruise the 25-minute walk home. Yeah. Maybe it'd even be good for him. And it wasn't rainin' or nothin'. Just cloudy. And Micah had nagged him enough, so he had his jacket to brave the numbingly chill 40° winds. Yeah, he'd be alright.

So Jake hitched his backpack strap over his right shoulder and began to hike. No one to walk with. The small fry from the elementary complex had already left. Whew! A bunch of guys were practicing b-ball in the gym. They'd be there for an hour yet. Nah, no one to walk with. But that's okay.

Now, Jake knew why he missed the bus today. And it wasn't the first time. Jeanie McCoy. Every Thursday she had a viola lesson after school. In the Music Hall. And she always took her time gettin' to her lesson. And Jake was still at his locker, jamming a couple of books into his pack. And she stopped to speak with . . . Jake. Oh, she had the kindest eyes. And the best smile. A musical, tingling voice. And mostly, she was . . . well, great.

So, today they really talked. About the skating party coming up next week. About the dumb history project. About Mr. Henson's mismatched socks. You know, a lot of good talkin'. And so Jake missed his bus.

But it wasn't so bad.

He had talked to Jeanie.

They were just friends. Jake wasn't about to get goofy over some girl. Just friends. But maybe they'd skate together a few times at the party. Jeanie seemed okay to that idea. And maybe he'd call her tomorrow or so, like after school. Just to talk. Yeah, like friends.

Jake smiled to himself. He sauntered across the street without really watching traffic. Some screaming maniac of a driver in a Ford Escort braked hard enough to sketch skid marks on the street. The grump yelled and honked at Jake. No sweat. He'd get over it. Right?

So Jake strode on.

And noticed a blister pickin' up on his left foot. Man, he had to get a better pair of socks! And why were his feet wet?

Then Jake stopped to look around him. Oh. It was raining! Kinda hard. Another ten minutes of this walkin' yet.

Awww! No!

Directions: Answer these questions.
1. What is Jake's initial problem? _____

   _____

2. How are these people connected to Jake?
   Micah   _____
   Jeanie   _____

3. What signs do we have that Jake daydreams on his walk?

   _____

   _____

4. Opinion: Does Jake like Jeanie more than just as a *friend?* State 3 reasons.

   _____

   _____

   _____

5. Give a synonym for each of these words or phrases.
   a. hissy fit   _____
   b. nagged   _____
   c. commenced   _____
   d. mismatched   _____

6. List three synonyms for *walk* or *walked* mentioned in the story.

   _____

7. The story carries the title "Just Friends." Give another appropriate title.

   _____

R U ->?

Follow these directions carefully:

1. Place the 12th and 19th letters of the alphabet in box 6.
2. In box 4 draw a feline face in the lower right corner.
3. Using word form, write the number for **12 - 3** in box 5.
4. In box 2 write the third letter of the alphabet.
5. Inscribe the word **BEHAVE** in box 4.
6. Place the interrogative punctuation after your letters in box 6.
7. Add **EATS** to the letter in box 2.
8. In box 3 write the word that completes this sentence: We played ten-pins at the bowling _____.
9. Write the word for **4 + 1** in box 6 between the two letters already placed there.
10. Place the 3-letter word for a female deer in box 1.
11. Delete the **E**'s in boxes 1, 2, and 3.
12. Move the first two letters in box 4 to the front of your word in box 3.
13. Delete the second letter in box 6.
14. In box 3 change the first letter to **R**.

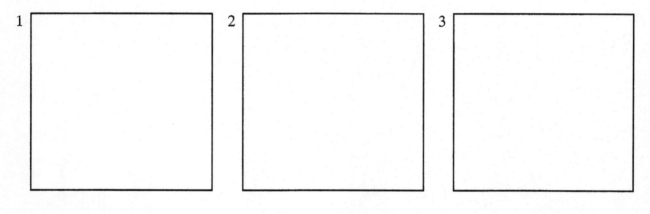

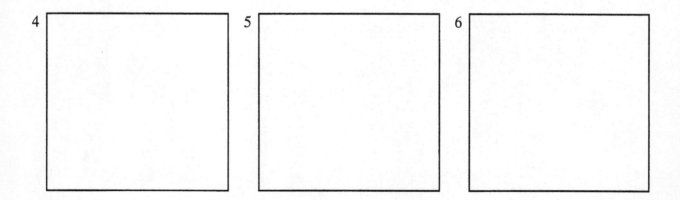

Niños y Niñas

Six children named Alberto, Bonita, Chantille, Dante, Ernesto, and Favi are playing in the Hernandez's yard. Name the three Hernandez children and list their ages.

1. If Favi isn't a Hernandez, Bonita is.
2. A Hernandez girl is older than her brother by two years.
3. The girl, Chantille, is 11.
4. If Alberto is a Hernandez, Ernesto is.
5. If Chantille isn't, Dante isn't.
6. A Hernandez boy is older than his sister by one year.
7. Favi is Dante's sister.
8. Chantille is the oldest child in her family.
9. Ernesto is 10.
10. The youngest of the six children is 9.

Child's Name	Age
_____	___
_____	___
_____	___

Tune Time Headlines

Match the headlines with the folklore lyrics.

Headlines:
a. Glad About That Feline Purchase!
b. Lost Love on Icy Mountain Top
c. The Pasta-Capped Horseman?
d. Gifts for the Quiet Toddler
e. Horse-Drawn Cart Approaches
f. Speedy Fire-Leaping Hans
g. Wealthy Ebony-Colored Ewe Gets Trim
h. Rodent-infested Time Piece
i. Swimming Farm Fowls
j. Wake up, Bro'! The Alarm is Sounding!
k. Digital Counting Game for the Elderly
l. Shropshire Acts as Mistress' Shadow

____ 1. Yankee Doodle went to town a'riding on his pony,
Stuck a feather in his hat and called it macaroni.

____ 2. Ducks in the millpond, a-geese in the clover,
A-fell in the millpond, a-wet all over.

____ 3. I bought me a cat. The cat pleased me.
I fed my cat under yonder tree. The cat went fiddle-i-fee.

____ 4. Hickory dickory dock. The mouse ran up the clock.
The clock struck one. The mouse ran down. Hickory dickory dock.

____ 5. Hush little baby, don't say a word,
Mama's goin' to buy you a mocking bird.

____ 6. Mary had a little lamb, its fleece was white as snow
And everywhere that Mary went the lamb was sure to go.

____ 7. On top of old Smoky, all covered with snow
I lost my true lover by courting too slow

____ 8. This old man, he played one. He played knick knack on my thumb.
Knick knack, paddy whack, give your dog a bone.
This old man came rolling home.

____ 9. Jack be nimble, Jack be quick.
Jack jumped over a candlestick.

____ 10. Swing low, sweet chariot, Comin' for to carry me home.
Swing low, sweet chariot, Comin' for to carry me home.

____ 11. Baa, baa, black sheep, have you any wool?
Yes sir, yes sir. Three bags full.

____ 12. Are you sleeping? Are you sleeping? Brother John. Brother John.
Morning bells are ringing. Morning bells are ringing.

Finishing Touches

Directions: Read each sentence fragment carefully. Wisely use words from the Word Bank to best complete each thought.

Word Bank		
practice	walk	sneeze
whimper	exercise	examine
grimace	comprehend	polish
share	sparkle	tighten
kindle	harmonize	exhaust
crave	heckle	

1. If Sean is pitched four balls, he will _____.
2. Because we were so cold coming indoors on that wintry eve, Tim brought in some wood to

   _____.
3. The silver tea set had lost its luster so Mama had me _____ it.
4. Because the puppy wished to go outdoors while we were all gone, she began to

   _____.
5. The four burly men with red-and-white striped shirts gathered around the piano player in order to let their voices _____.
6. The lab technician set the sample beneath the microscope to _____ the tissue sample.
7. Without the Triple Q Decoder which he left in his glove compartment, the secret agent could not _____ the message.
8. As allergic as Katey is to cats, it's no surprise that she would _____.
9. Feeling sorry for the child beggar, my brother cut his sandwich in half so that he might

   _____ it.
10. The wolf followed the wounded caribou for five miles in an effort to _____ his chosen prey.
11. The lemonade was so sour that Fern could not help but _____. What a face!
12. Thinking his son was another Mozart, Jean Baptiste Kloppelmeier ordered the child to pick up his tambourine and _____ it.
13. Having no chance to buy chocolate candy, the astronaut did _____ that mouth-watering treat.
14. Toothy Tanya brushes her dental work so that her teeth _____.
15. The governmental candidate became red-faced when a rowdy and unforgiving activist began to _____ him.
16. The juice sloshed out of the glass bottle because Shannon forgot to _____ its lid.

Hide-and-Seek

Directions: Read the selection below and answer the following questions.

As Bill started to count, Scotty scooted off as fast as his four-year-old legs could carry him.

"Not in the house. Not in the house," Scotty muttered to himself. He was excited. He was completely into the game. He was so happy he almost . . . well . . . he almost wet himself!

Bill, his older brother, had agreed to play hide-and-seek with Scotty. Now, that didn't happen often anymore. Since he entered middle school, Bill had less time for his young brother. He liked him. Sure. He just spent more time with the guys from school.

Bill counted slowly and loudly so that Scotty could hear him better. When he reached 25, he stopped.

"Hmm! I wonder where that little booger is" Bill exclaimed in a playful, wise older-sibling voice.

"Is he in here?" Bill queried as he opened the door to Scotty's junk-laden, clothing-strewn, chaotic, and musty closet. "Uh-h-h, nope!"

Well, that was strange. Scotty always began the hide-and-seek game with a dive into this hole. Hm. Must be growin' tired of it. I know I am, thought Bill.

Next Bill searched through his own bedroom, Dad and Mom's room, and the laundry area—especially the clothes dryer. Mom **forbade** that hideout. But with Scotty you never knew. Nope, not there. Not in the dirty-clothes basket either.

Bill opened the front entry closet. Nope. Under the dining room table. Uh-uh. Inside the base of the piano. Nada. Zipped up within the green beanbag chair? Nah!

"Say, Ma. Any idea where Scotty's hiding?" There was just a touch of worry in Bill's question.

Ma's mouth puckered into a playful half-smile. "Oh? Is Scotty getting any better at hiding?"

"He must be! I've looked around for more than ten minutes. I don't think Scotty can keep this hiding stuff up much longer."

"Well, I thought I heard the door open. Why don't you check outdoors?"

"What? He never goes out there! He's afraid of the bogey man. Ever since Dad told him that scary story on the camp-out last summer."

"Well, someone opened the door. Go and take a look!" urged Ma.

"Okay . . . ."

Bill chuckled to himself. Scotty outside! A miracle. Bill strolled off toward the play fort, abandoned the past five months due to a colorful storytelling and a fright-filled imagination. But Scotty wasn't there. Not in the garbage can either.

When Scotty was younger, Bill often carried him to the curb in the garbage can, muttering about the heavy load, pretending the young boy was trash. Oh-h, the boys had fun with that! And Mr. Cummings, the mail carrier, noticed the boys while walking his route. Mr. Cummings still called Scotty "Rubbish Rat."

But Scotty wasn't there.

Not in the garage. The lilac bushes were child-free.

How odd!

Then Bill heard it.

Not quite a wail. More like a moan.

"Ohh, Bill . . . Bill. Oh-h! Oh-h! I-ma stuck!"

Bill glided to the street side of the house. Yup, there! Up in the sugar maple tree which bordered the street. About ten feet up. A small blue-jean-clad blob sat. Yeah. Red coat, redder-faced. A bit of wetness glistening on the cheeks.

"Hey, Scotty! You okay?"

"No-o-oh! I'm-m-ma stuck, Bill. Can ya get me out? Please!"

The kid was speaking softly. He usually did. But if Bill didn't say or do just the right thing, that soft moan would change. And the tears would flow again!

"Okay, kiddo. Here I come. Wow! What a great hiding place!"

Up, up, up clambered Scotty's hero.

Questions:

1. Who are the main characters? _____

2. What game do the boys play? _____

3. Give a synonym for **forbade**. _____

4. Why didn't Bill think Scotty would be outdoors?_____

5. Why does Scotty have the nickname "Rubbish Rat"? _____

   _____

6. What is the "bit of wetness"? _____

7. Thought questions: Why do younger children like to play with older kids? Why is this a healthy thing?

   _____

   _____

   _____

   _____

Look the Whole World Over

Each of the rebuses below is the name of a city of the world. Write the name of the city on the first blank. Write the name of the continent on which the city is located on the second blank.

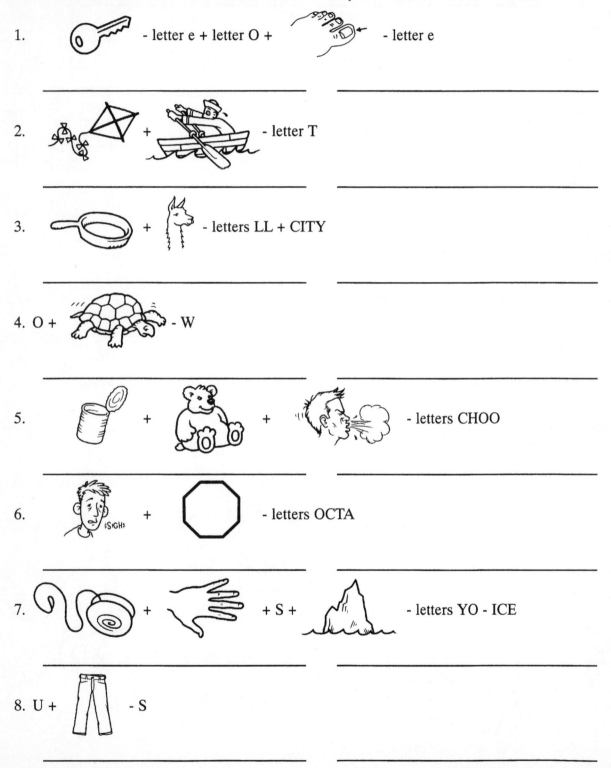

1. [key] - letter e + letter O + [thumb] - letter e

_____   _____

2. [kite] + [man rowing boat] - letter T

_____   _____

3. [pan] + [llama] - letters LL + CITY

_____   _____

4. O + [turtle] - W

_____   _____

5. [can] + [bear] + [man blowing] - letters CHOO

_____   _____

6. [man sighing *SIGH*] + [octagon] - letters OCTA

_____   _____

7. [hose] + [hand] + S + [iceberg] - letters YO - ICE

_____   _____

8. U + [jeans] - S

_____   _____

Togetherness

What words do you think of when you hear the numbered words below? Match each with its partner from the Word Bank.

Word Bank

dine	Gretel	subtract	fro	Q's	cheese	tell	jelly	repel
fall	roll	eggs	saucer	winter	doom	Clark	there	stretch
dance	goats	shut	Indian	Odyssey	south	foot	conquer	Eve

1. open & _____
2. bend & _____
3. Hansel & _____
4. hand & _____
5. French & _____
6. song & _____
7. Iliad & _____
8. wine & _____
9. sheep & _____
10. bacon & _____
11. north & _____
12. Adam & _____
13. rock & _____
14. macaroni & _____

15. rise & _____
16. gloom & _____
17. summer & _____
18. P's & _____
19. attract & _____
20. divide & _____
21. show & _____
22. Lewis & _____
23. to & _____
24. add & _____
25. peanut butter & _____
26. here & _____
27. cup & _____

Ripping Jamjams

A week before Christmas, Tommy started it. He took hold of my increasingly thin, wear-worn, cowboy-decorated jamjams and *yanked*.

R-r-r-rip!

"Hey, whatcha do that for?" I cried.

"Aw, come on, Chubs. Ya know Grandma's makin' us new ones. We'll get 'em at the Christmas Eve party."

"Yeah, you're right, I guess," I admitted slowly.

So I grabbed hold of the *elastic* waistband of Tommy's jamjams. I gave it a well-deserved, *thorough* stretch test. Yup! Poor quality. They tore.

It snowed that night. It snowed every night that week, and school was out for the holidays. By day we sledded down Big Ditch Hill. By night we watched *goofy* Christmas specials and in the *confines* of our bedroom tore our jamjams. After all, we'd get new ones. Grandma made new ones every year.

Every Christmas Eve uncles and aunts returned to the farm for this gathering. Cousins of *assorted* shapes and sizes, cousins I did not recognize, came and sat hip to hip with us as we *anticipated* the gifts we'd receive. Oh, it was more blessed to give than to receive. But, man, what would we get?

So all week long we were on pins and needles.

Mama made up eggnog one day. It was kinda *potent*. And it sure was different. Aunt Barb showed us how to make *taffy*. Pulling taffy!

Oh, we had a big snowball fight, too. All the neighbor kids came and clustered by our barn that Thursday afternoon. We built forts, piled our crystallized ammo, avoided the road apples left by the farm's horses, and planned our *martial* strategies. Lots of fun.

We tore our jamjams some more that night.

On Friday we had a sled pull. Dad tied ropes from our toboggans and sleds to the tire-chained tractor. He also drove like Jehu. We fairly flew through the fields and orchards. We *soared* over ditches, played chicken with the passing mailboxes, and side-swiped each other as we *vied* for the honor of having the reddest, the coldest, the frostiest face.

And that night we had our last jamjam rip session.

Good thing. Our jamjams were pert near memories. Tommy had no buttons on his top. The back of his shirt consisted of three strips hanging from a collar. His pants were only half their original length and hung from the waistband by three threads. My jams, too, were *marred*. No left arm. Pants split. My fly hole went clear around the crotch. I coulda worn the pants backwards without knowing. Boy, it was a good thing Grandma was making those new jamjams!

On Saturday afternoon our family piled into the car. Smells of casseroles, desserts, and breads were thick. I warmed my hands on the Tater Tot dish Mama had me hold in my lap.

We were *beckoned* to Grandma's house by the blue-lighted, five-pointed star which hung from the windmill over their water pump. When we scooted into the house, we were greeted by what seemed to be half of the world's human creation. The kitchen counters were loaded with pies, bars, meats, hot dishes, sweet rolls, Jell-Os, buttered veggies, pitchers of milk.

You know how adults toy with you? How they tease you *unmercifully*? No presents 'til supper was over! And supper always took a *millennium*. Or two. And Uncle Dale made it longer. Grandpa loved to tell stories. Every time he'd say, "Well, is it time now?" Uncle Dale would butt in, "Hey, Dad, tell about the time . . . ." You know. Over and over again. And every time he'd get Grandpa to tell another story, Dale'd grin, look over at Tommy and me, and wink!

I coulda killed him.

Finally Grandpa stopped talking. Grandma *shoveled* us all into the living room where the Christmas tree took over the far end. You could hardly see the tree because of all the presents. Gazillions of relatives require loads of gifts.

Seemed to take forever. I got a good plaid shirt from my cousin Sandy. Tommy a plastic bow and arrow from Cousin Dave. Looked like it'd been played with a couple of times already. Finally our names were called off together. A package from Grandma. We just smiled. Oh, yeah. It's jamjam time again.

So together we unwrapped our gift. Slowly, *savoring* the final moments. We stole glances at Grandma who smiled ever-so-humbly in her rocker. Finally, Tommy pulled off the last of the paper, and there . . . lay four pairs of Christmas socks, two coloring books, and a small box of Crayola crayons.

"Thanks, Gramma!" we said as enthusiastically as we could manage.

Grandma never made us another pair of Christmas jamjams. After Mama discovered the state of our nightly wear, she wore us out. She got us store-bought pajamas. And we were rosy-cheeked without going outdoors.

Directions: Match the phrases below with their italicized synonyms from the story.

1. strong _____	10. without pity _____
2. 1,000 years _____	11. warlike _____
3. easy to stretch _____	12. of many varieties _____
4. ruined _____	13. competed _____
5. awaiting excitedly _____	14. a private place _____
6. complete _____	15. pushed _____
7. called by signal _____	16. pulled _____
8. a chewing candy _____	17. expected _____
9. kiddie or childish _____	18. flew _____

Hidden Treasures

Each pair of words or phrases below hides two smaller words which are related in some manner. For example, the word pair **wealth, youth** hides the words *we* and *you*. Find the related words in the problems below.

1. toilsome, spaniel _____ _____

2. expend, winking _____ _____

3. clearly, globe _____ _____

4. no value, grounder _____ _____

5. shootist, growling _____ _____

6. scarred, automatic _____ _____

7. chairman, cutlery _____ _____

8. scolding, swindle _____ _____

9. shower, stellar _____ _____

10. horsewhip, to need less _____ _____

11. reminding, smattering _____ _____

12. simplify, bookshelf _____ _____

13. comedian, pagoda _____ _____

14. rambling, jewelry _____ _____

15. design, imposter _____ _____

16. Tennessee, Popeye _____ _____

17. sunken, crayon _____ _____

18. marmalade, cutlasses _____ _____

19. endanger, madrigal _____ _____

20. franchise, scowl _____ _____

21. slovenly, phosphates _____ _____

22. bridegroom, carbuncle _____ _____

23. combine, armchair _____ _____

24. rebate, balloon _____ _____

Can It Get Any Better?

Replace the underlined words with the appropriate words below.

chap	investigator	pretentious	bellowing	palpitate	jade,
mirth	horde	flicker	detritus	carafe	bistro
andante	umber	turret	repel	exploits	demise

As I sit outside a 1 <u>small restaurant</u> in the village of Gagne, I must share a moment of 2 <u>laughter,</u> recalling my recent 3 <u>feats.</u>

You see, I am the famous 4 <u>researcher</u>, Jean LeSimpe! Yes, I am the one who rediscovered the Angolan 5 <u>woodpecker.</u> And the brave soul who survived the 50-foot drop from a 6 <u>small tower</u> outside Amsterdam. Ah, I can see your heart is beginning to 7 <u>throb</u> as you recall the *Washington Post's* story of my escape from the pile of 8 <u>loose rock fragments</u> as a 9 <u>large crowd</u> of 10 <u>superior-assuming</u> snobs planned my 11 <u>ruin.</u>

Yes, as I pour myself a drink from this 12 <u>glass bottle</u> and play the 13 <u>moderately slow</u> movement from my beloved Verdi's *Mass,* I am indeed thankful. If not for the mysterious young 14 <u>fellow</u> in the 15 <u>brown-</u> and-16 <u>green</u>-colored topcoat who drove into the midst of that 17 <u>screaming</u> crowd, I would not have been able to 18 <u>drive back</u> their ringleaders with my trusty umbrella.

Some day I shall tell you the entire story.

1. _____
2. _____
3. _____
4. _____
5. _____
6. _____
7. _____
8. _____
9. _____
10. _____
11. _____
12. _____
13. _____
14. _____
15. _____
16. _____
17. _____
18. _____

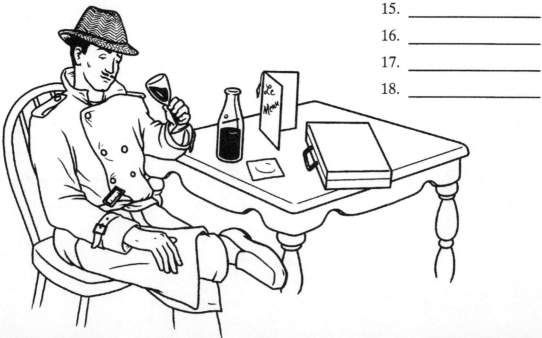

Rivalry

Read the story. Then complete the story map.

Katie is steaming! Two days ago, Gwen, her 20-year-old sister, had come home from college. Gwen spent the night finishing off all the ice cream in the fridge and camping out in front of the TV all evening so Katie and her best friend Kimberly couldn't watch the video they had rented. And then yesterday morning, Gwen waltzed off to college taking Katie's winter coat! And December gets cold in Wisconsin.

So yesterday went like this:

"Mom, guess what! You're gonna hafta get me another winter coat!"

"Dream on, hon."

"But Gwen **snitched** mine."

"That's interesting. Call her up to see what's up."

So she did. Katie was even **civil**. Or she would have been. Unfortunately, Katie merely got Big Sister's answering machine. At the tone she entered:

"Hey, Duffel Brain, it's your sister. Gimme my coat or I'll trash your bedroom. You won't even recognize it when you come back for the holidays. [Then sweetly chiming . . . .] Oh, our number is 1-920-881-9005. Have a nice day!"

There! That oughta get her going, Katie thought.

But it didn't. Katie waited by the phone all afternoon. Got a call from Ted. Wanted to see a movie. Dream on, Teddy Bear! Got another call from Kimber. Yeah, the mall would be good for tomorrow afternoon if Mom okays it. Some pet shelter called for donations. Nope, no financial support this year. Yeah, it's worthy but family's spending money on hurricane victims. Yeah, uh huh, uh huh. Sure. Good luck. Bye.

She waited for Gwen's call all evening, even holding off on walking the dog until late that night. She pulled on her dad's sweatshirt and her mom's scarf. Felt like Bob Cratchit. Boy, was it **nippy**!

So when Gwen still hadn't returned her call this morning, Katie smiled grimly. She waited until Mom went out on her errands.

"Vengeance is mine!" Katie roared. She entered Princess Gwenyth's **hallowed** hall and trashed the place. She upended the half-full waste basket. She strategically placed bluish-brown, rotting bananas under the bed covers. All clothing hanging in the closet was pulled down, making a mound below. She soaped "To my thoughtful, thieving thithter" on Gwen's **vanity** mirror. After unscrewing all light bulbs, Katie left the room, closing the door behind her.

At noon, Mom returned.

"Look, hon! Look what I got for Gwen!"

Oh, great. It was a new winter coat.

"But she's got *mine*," cried Katie enviously.

"Oh, I'm sure you'll get yours back soon. Did you get through to Gwen when you called yesterday?"

"No, I . . . ."

"Hello, everyone! I'm back!"

Gwen stepped into the house.

"Hi, dear," sang Mom cheerily.

"I got your coat, Katie. Sorry! I should've asked you first. Here you go." And Gwen dumped the coat into Katie's lap.

"I gotta get something from my room and my driver's waiting in the car, so I gotta make this quick. Be right back!" chattered Big Sister.

Katie dropped her head onto the table.

There was a **canine-like** howl.

"Mom! What happened to my room?"

Mom's quick steps **clipped** down the hallway.

Silence.

"Katie, what on earth did you do . . .? Get in here now, child. You are in serious trouble."

Story Title: _____

Characters: _____ _____ _____

Time: _____   Place: _____

Opening Problem: _____

Five Main Events: 1. _____

                                      2. _____

                                      3. _____

                                      4. _____

                                      5. _____

Closing Problem: _____

Possible Solution: _____

words and meanings: (Use context clues to determine their meanings.)

snitched _____

civil _____

nippy _____

hallowed _____

vanity _____

canine-like _____

clipped _____

Can You Make Heads or Tails out of It?

Directions: Below are illustrations of nine idioms. Figure them out and write them on the blanks.

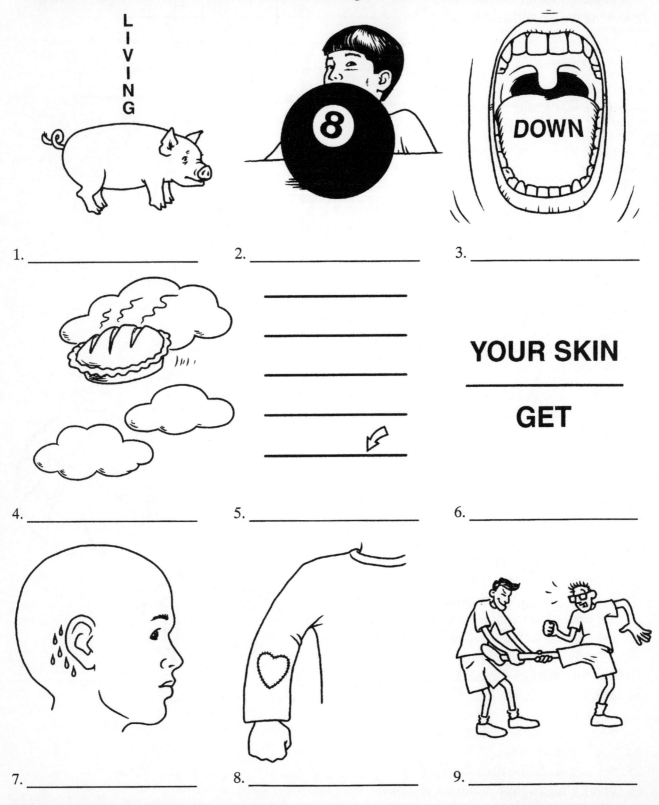

1. _____

2. _____

3. _____

4. _____

5. _____

6. _____

7. _____

8. _____

9. _____

Going for the Gold

Fill in the grid with words
matching the definitions below.

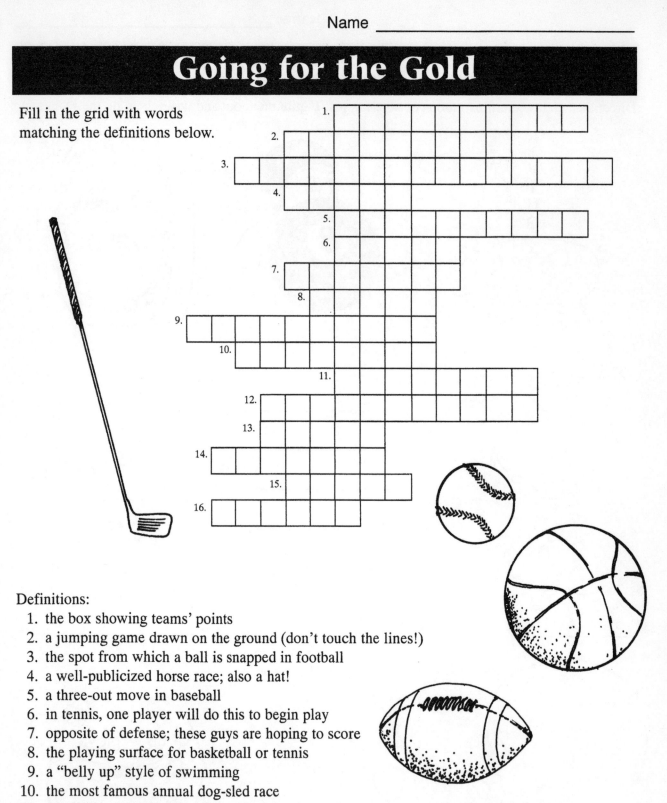

Definitions:
1. the box showing teams' points
2. a jumping game drawn on the ground (don't touch the lines!)
3. the spot from which a ball is snapped in football
4. a well-publicized horse race; also a hat!
5. a three-out move in baseball
6. in tennis, one player will do this to begin play
7. opposite of defense; these guys are hoping to score
8. the playing surface for basketball or tennis
9. a "belly up" style of swimming
10. the most famous annual dog-sled race
11. originally a Native American team sport now played with a small ball and netted bat
12. or Ping-Pong
13. a hard slam in volleyball
14. spear-tossing event
15. the human club-carrier for a golfer
16. many athletes (like soccer players) wear these shoes for grip

Time Is on Your Side

Directions: Below are three scenes. Unfortunately, the events for each scene are out of order. Please number the events 1 through 7 in correct chronological order.

Scene 1: Sondra, the social butterfly, wants to put on a party in the worst way. This is what should happen these last two days:

_____ write down the names of kids to invite to the party

_____ take out a pen and paper

_____ remind guests what time to come

_____ Mom said it was time to plan a guest list

_____ show list to and get okay from Dad

_____ number this paper from one to ten

_____ call guests to invite them to the party

Scene 2: Bob, the boisterous basketball bad-boy, was warned by Coach to be ready for practice today. Strangely enough, Bob is. He did the following:

_____ retrieved clothes from locker

_____ remembered (for once) to take gym bag to school

_____ stashed bag in locker

_____ emptied the clothes drier of sports clothes in evening

_____ changed into gym clothes

_____ stayed awake for all classes to avoid detentions

_____ packed gym bag to take tomorrow

Scene 3: Theodora, the dramatic debutante, hoped this Halloween would be the best one yet. On October 31, she was a whirlwind of energy. She. . .

_____ returned home because she forgot a treat bag.

_____ got into her costume when her face was ready.

_____ chose a costume idea in the morning.

_____ in mid-afternoon bought warts, glasses, and gory make-up from the local pharmacy.

_____ went to the store to buy a wig at noon.

_____ stood before a mirror to put on facial make-up.

_____ eagerly left the house to glean the snacking goods.

Farmer Questions Chicken IQ

The Disassociated Press

HENGAARD, North Dakota—A poultry farmer in this remote community 50 miles west of Bismarck made a startling discovery last Thursday as he inspected one of his hen coops. His chickens were raising their own livestock.

"In one corner of the coop, the biddies had set up a box of beetles," said Bert DeHaan. "I guess they've fed them [beetles] grain from their own mix. Can't say I ever saw anything like it before. No, this is a real corker."

According to Shannon Scratch, inspector for the state agriculture administration, the chickens had also developed a cockroach ranch, an ant colony, and a mealworm pit. When asked how long the hens had farmed these smaller creatures, Ms. Scratch offered no comment. Neither would she comment when asked about the intelligence of the chickens.

Mr. DeHaan believes the chickens are able to build these insect pens with their beaks, coordinate community goals, and plan insect harvests. He says, "The chickens are raising the bugs for food. No doubt about it. I've seen them herd them, separate the fattened critters, and gobble them down like they were having a feast." Records show that egg production in this coop has improved by 23% in the past 18 months, far above the production of other coops.

When asked how smart his flock was, DeHaan smiled and shrugged his shoulders. "Don't know for sure, but can't be as dumb as some folks around here. You know, there's been talk of an alien landing around these parts . . . ."

Fill in the blanks below.

1. Two people are interviewed in this article. Who are they?

   _____   _____

2. What is the main idea of this article?   _____

   _____

3. When did this event occur?   _____

4. In what state did this happen?   _____

5. Name three additional claims the farmer made.

   _____

   _____

   _____

The Escape

Into the shady glen the small figure rode on a pony little larger than a dog. The pony's breath misted in the crisp air as the beast blew air out of its nostrils. The green-mantled figure patted the neck of the beast, whispering words of comfort into the animal's ear. In response the faithful steed nickered, thumped his wide hoofs twice upon the soft bed of the forest floor, and ceased its shaking.

"We've left the raiders behind, old friend," said Rowan, as she removed her hooded mantle and tossed her head back and forth, bringing peace to her own troubled mind. Rowan was not human. She was neither elfin nor dwarf of story tales. Nay, she was a mystic, one of four daughters of Sylvia, guide of all wood folk.

Suddenly shouts of rough men and screams of abused war horses cut through the glade's peace.

"In here, ol' churl, I tell ya. The maid's gone to hidin' in this grove."

"Nah, ya lunk. She'd never wait for us here. Not after she dunked old Stefan at the marsh. Noo! She's a gone on to her crazy folk, don'tcha know."

The two grey-cloaked riders dismounted, still arguing as they examined the earth for traces of the maiden's flight.

"Who was the lout who let her escape?" asked the first.

"'Tis one who no longer breathes the air so freely," returned the second grimly. "The lord beheaded the fool by scimitar even as the knave begged for mercy. Ah, there's little patience for one who lets a mystic escape, to be true!"

Five nobly-dressed horsemen wove through the trees to the clearing where these two rustics still squatted. In the lead came the fierce lord, a huge form with scarlet and grey finery worn over his coat of mail.

"What say you?" he roared. "Have ye found the trail of Rowan?"

"No, sire," spoke the first grey, trembling, "though I was certain the child headed into this wood. Shall I continue to search, lord?"

"Aye, indeed," replied the master calmly, controlled. "She is here, I know it too. You have a keen sense for the hunt, Mikkel. Be at ready with your blade. And you too, Short Brush! Though a child, our Rowan is vicious with her weapon."

"Yes, sire," agreed Mikkel and Short Brush.

The two greys beat the bushes in the search. Closer and closer they came to the child's hiding place, a small earthen scoop created when the roots of a wind-blown tree pulled free of the earth.

The evil lord and his lot remained mounted, ready to pursue should the young girl determine to take flight once more.

And so they were not prepared for the child's play.

Rowan softly, softly sang, "You wind-whipped branches shudder, shake. You oaks and cedars tremble, take these men and beasts who do us wrong. Not in these woods do they belong."

As a mighty gust of wind roared, nearby trees slapped their branches to the point of breaking, as they reached out and grasped the five mounted men. An immense gaping cavern opened in the trunk of an ancient oak and swallowed the five surprised mail-clad men whole before closing and crushing the evil ones.

Mikkel and Short Brush too were lifted high into the air by a white pine and a blue spruce. Lifted high. Kept high. For awhile.

"Return from whence you came. Go to your families and tell them of the wrath of Sylvia," commanded Rowan. "She would not you to her land come again!"

The pine and spruce tossed the two grey trackers over the trees of the forest and into the field beyond. A field already harvested and soggy with the rains of autumn. Mikkel and Short Brush, unhurt but shaken by their arboreal flight, rose and fled immediately to tell their missus of the strange doings of this wood.

The child Rowan gathered the reins of her pony, climbed on to her mount, and turned her beast toward her mother's lodge, a mere three days travel.

"I come," she softly called.

Answer these questions.

1. What sort of creature is Rowan? _____

2. What do we know of her kind so far? _____

3. How many enemy are mentioned in this selection? _____

4. How do we know of the power of Rowan? _____

5. Imagine. Why might the evil lord wish to recapture Rowan?

    _____

    _____

6. What is the meaning of the word *arboreal*.

    _____

7. Why might Rowan have allowed the two rustics to remain alive?

    _____

    _____

8. What season of the year is it? _____

I'll File Away

Last Friday Francine's fuchsia-colored filing cabinet flew out her twelfth-floor window. Fortunately, Fran's 32 file entries survived the fall. Help her put each word file back into its correct folder.

Francine's 32 file entries:
applaud, ebony, anvil, compliment, cookies, amber, fir, fire, lira, CD, pie, acacia, honey, candle, peso, aquamarine, rock, violin, banyan, yen, exalt, elephant, crimson, baseball, tamarack, rupee, Monopoly, laud, match, bar bell, candy cane, torch

colors

money

things that
light

things you
play

sweets

words for
praise

trees

heavy stuff

Are You Conning Me?

Complete each sentence with a *con-* word from the Word Bank.

Word Bank					
converged	controversy	contorted	constable	conclude	consult
content	convince	conduct	concertina	conscious	congested
confetti	contrition	contestant	conservation	conjures	confabulate

1. The mall was _____ with swarms of sale-crazed customers.

2. Did you _____ your teacher that Kool-Aid is a food group?

3. Please _____ your doctor if your fever continues.

4. Peter's face _____ in pain as his horse stomped on his foot.

5. The two highways _____ before we reached Toronto.

6. I despise those who _____ and gossip, destroying the peace and goodwill of our grand community, Gotham City.

7. Our _____ group hopes to plant 50 trees this Saturday.

8. The tearful toddler, filled with _____, told her dead goldfish that she only meant to take it for a walk.

9. Are you _____, Henry? Speak to me if you can hear me!

10. The brawny guide will _____ us to the bottom of the gorge.

11. Our meeting will _____ in 20 minutes.

12. There was a horrid _____ about the music selection chosen for the skating party.

13. What evil the wicked warlock _____ against his unsuspecting apprentice!

14. When the first _____ could not answer the riddle, he was sentenced to nine years hard dishwashing.

15. After our team won, we tossed _____ high into the air to celebrate.

16. My cousin Vinnie played "The Blue Danube" on his _____ until his mother tossed it into the river.

17. Hans was not _____ with his gingerbread cookie. He wanted the whole house!

18. The _____ would not arrest Bo Peep for crying at the park.

Queen of the Heap

Whenever we had a hankerin' for somethin' to do, all we had to do was mosey on outside. Ya see, my family lived out in the country, and we had the whole world for our playground. And there were still lots of kids to play with. The twins lived just across the road from us. The Peretti boys, the Botts, and Mary Lou McCastle all lived within easy walkin' distance.

In the wintertime we could sled down Killer Hill, build snow forts behind the Perettis' chicken coop, skate on the twins' pond, or play Dog-and-Deer in somebody's yard. Our parents knew us all, fed us all, paddled us all on occasion, and compared kid notes with each other after Sunday services.

We could sled for hours. We'd pull on a couple pairs of pants, three or more sweaters, floppy-eared hat and hooded coat, mittens with spares for the pockets, insulated boots with four pairs of socks, and the needful scarf. No way would we get cold! After flying down Killer Hill on our steel-runner Flexible Flyers or all-metal Flying Saucers, we'd expend all our energy trudgin' back up to the hilltop. Oh, we sometimes crashed into each other—meanin' to, of course—or into that gnarly, monster apple tree we called Mr. Scrooge—not meanin' to!—and take a few minutes to catch our breaths again. But we could play for hours, lose five pounds through sweat and exercise, and each return to his homestead with wind-reddened face, snow-soaked clothes, frozen fingers and toes, and a hope to return again. More sooner than later.

My older sister Leanne was often out there with the rest of us. Now whatever we did, she could do better. If I landed safely after a fly over our jumbo ski jump, she'd be sure to jump farther and land better. If we built a snow fort, she'd build a castle. If some fool broke her record for sliding the longest distance, she'd break that record anew by another good ten feet.

Well, Pop got a Scorpion snowmobile that winter. It wasn't needed but sure was fun. We'd fairly fly through the fields on that noisy contraption with wintry winds whippin' all sensation from our air-exposed cheeks. Eyes would water great tears, which collected and froze on our ice-hardened scarves. Pop rigged a toggle to the rear of the snowmobile so we could be pulled on skis and sleds. Well, once we got our Scorpion, Leanne thought she'd make the best snowmobiler in three counties. And she was probably right!

Leanne could lazy-eight that snow machine with a clean cut Scottie Hamilton couldn't match. She could slalom through the young apple trees better than Peek-a-Boo Street. We'd marvel at her performance, more than a little jealous of her mobile magic.

But on Tuesday we were sleddin' Killer Hill again. We had an icy run that day because of Monday's mid-thirties heat wave. This glaze was covered by a two-inch blanket of fluff. The Hill was faster, slicker, and deadlier than ever and we loved it! Well, we were just a'slidin' away when Leanne came a'roarin' up the hill on the Scorpion, scatterin' us small fry like milkweed seeds. She wasn't even payin' any attention to us. No, she was yankin' at her scarf, which had been sucked into the air intake of her snowmobile. First with one hand, then with both, Leanne pulled on her unfortunate scarf, heedless of the wind and weather—or us who shared time and space with her.

Finally, with one tremendous jerk, Leanne freed her frayed fleece. In doin' so she lost her balance and toppled off the left side of the Scorpion which was speedin' nigh unto 57 mph. Well, that snowmobile wobbled to the left; it leaned to the right; it tilted to the left again, and . . . tipped over.

But it didn't conk out. No sirree! Somehow, Leanne done froze the throttle in place with her hell-bent, high-speed, mobilistical shenanigans. That machine, off on its left side with treads spinning crazily, attemptin' to grip the snow but merely skimmin' the icy glaze, completed donuts around the fallen form of my stunned-to-silence sister.

Around and around sped the riderless steed, a snowmobile unmastered and unmistressed. Finally tired of its mundane donut-making, the tread-spinnin' machine righted itself, got its bearings, and roared across the gravel road toward the twins' cow barn.

"No! Not the barn!" wailed Neddy and Teddy in perfect tutti voice.

The Scorpion heard their prayer. It veered to the right, narrowly missin' the corner of the barn, and slammed head-on into a large, pungent pile of cow poop, where it ceased its engine clatter with one mighty whoomp!

Leanne slowly rose to her feet. She flashed her haughty, queenly smile at us and crowed, "Bet'cha couldn't do that trick!"

She was right, of course. We couldn't.

Complete these cause-and-effect sentences.

1. Because Pop rigged up a toggle on the snowmobile,

   _____.

2. Because of Monday's warmer temperature,

   _____.

3. Because we had many neighbors and the world was our playground,

   _____.

4. Because the unmanned snowmobile was heading for the barn,

   _____.

5. Because her scarf was sucked into the air intake,

   _____.

6. Because _____,
   the snowmobile's engine stopped.

7. Because _____,
   Leanne built a castle of snow.

8. Because _____,
   the Scorpion spun circles around Leanne.

9. Who are you more like, the author or Leanne? Name two ways.

   _____.

10. Could this story happen? _____ Give a reason for your answer.

   _____.

A Moral Dilemma

A couple of years ago, Wesley Kidd and his family lived in Central America. Both of his parents taught in an English-speaking school there, and Wesley was able to learn Spanish with the aid of eager classmates. Wes enjoyed living in new surroundings. He met new people, made new friends, appreciated the world experience.

But Wesley was troubled much of the time. This Latin American country was so poor! In the large city below his home lived some wealthy families. They had large, well-groomed mansions, walled homes, great luxuries. There also lived many poor people in their simple homes. Some were mud and brick, some wooden slabs, some cardboard or corrugated metal. Many homes had dirt floors. No electricity. Kids of these homes might have jobs of walking to the community well to haul water back to their houses. The rich had servants, gardens, cars, clothing, plenty. The poor had . . . well, what did they have?

A few months earlier, before Wes and his family went to this land, they took classes called "orientation workshops." They were told what to expect in this country. Many beggars. Don't give them money, warned their trainer. It keeps them begging, he said. Begging doesn't teach people how to be constructive members of society. And parents may force kids to beg. That's wrong, he said.

Maybe so. But sometimes Wesley became very uncomfortable seeing such poverty. There was a little girl in a blue dress who sold flowers with her blind grandmother. The girl, maybe seven or eight years old, took care of all the money from their sales. She always smiled. But she had such big, dark eyes. And she looked kinda frail. And sometimes Wesley and his family rode through the city by bus or taxi. They could see lame people. One man had no legs at all. He sat on a wheeled cart about the size of home plate, and he pushed himself around with his calloused knuckles. Wes saw him at a market one day and was sure those impatient taxi drivers would run him over when he crossed the busy street.

But the worst feeling Wesley Kidd got happened when he'd eat at a restaurant. You see, the poor people couldn't afford to eat at such places but the rich folks ate out all the time. Tourist North Americans always ate out. One day a young woman beggar with two babies, one still an infant, begged for food as the Kidds left a Popeye's restaurant. Wes's mom gave her a chicken leg and a cup of mashed potatoes. Another time Wesley was seated out on a restaurant patio, chowing down on a Burger King Whopper when he heard a whispered plea. Two dirty hands stretched out through some foliage and a small Hispanic boy's voice called, "Por favor! Por favor!" A store manager heard the pleas, stomped on over to the beggar's hideout, and sternly ordered the urchin to leave. Using words Wes couldn't understand.

And Wesley still cannot understand. How come North Americans are so rich? he wonders. Do we deserve to be better off than others? What could I have done for hungry people? Why is life so . . . so unfair?

Wes sits at his desk daydreaming. He's wearing a sweater and jeans. He has on a pair of name-brand shoes. He turns to see his class computer station. The room hums as the air control unit blows out a steady stream of comfortable and comforting warm air. His stomach growls, telling him that it is about time to eat. He imagines he will eat only half the food he gets at the school food service. Probably throw away the rest.

It's alright in the United States. Or is it?

Questions

1. Circle the words which describe Wesley.   loud   thoughtful   happy

    hateful   timid   concerned   greedy   sleepy   honest

2. What is Wesley's main concern? _____

    _____

3. According to Wes' instructor, why should people give beggars no money?

    _____

4. Describe in three phrases the young child at Burger King.

    _____   _____

    _____

5. Think about this. How are Americans wasteful?

    _____

    _____

    _____

6. If you were Wes's older sister or brother, what suggestions would you make to help him with his concern? _____

    _____

    _____

    _____

    _____

It's in Plain English

Match these phrases with their corresponding pictures.

1. a monarch hoofing it _____
2. a grenadier faltering _____
3. a dodecagon sweltering _____
4. a thespian orating _____
5. a magistrate prevaricating _____
6. a tsunami elevating _____
7. a mustang rearing _____
8. a carbuncle glittering _____

9. maize flourishing _____
10. a nematode burrowing _____
11. a mariner navigating _____
12. a tibia fracturing _____
13. a coleoptera masticating _____
14. a herald thundering _____
15. a trekker snoozing _____

a. 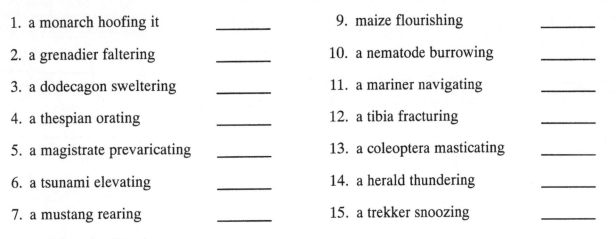 b. c. d. e.

f.  g.  h.  i.  j.

k. 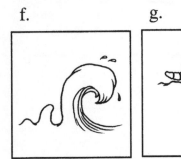 l.  m.  n.  o.

Like, for Sure!

Each of these sentences is unlikely, perhaps even impossible. Explain why.

1. The deaf man caught us whispering in the darkened theater.

   _____

2. The omnipotent ruler of Zanzibar could not thread the needle.

   _____

3. We live in the vacant house across from the train station.

   _____

4. "To infinity and beyond!" shouted Buzz.

   _____

5. We silently left to hide behind the corner of the barn silo.

   _____

6. Does a big, scary ghost live in your bedroom?

   _____

7. The red, large-combed rooster lay three eggs last week.

   _____

8. The minuscule rodent towered over us.

   _____

9. The carnivorous, malevolent snake lived on grapes, tubers, and grains.

   _____

10. I exist in a deep, dark void.

   _____

11. The Hereford bull gave birth to a gangly young calf.

   _____

12. We saw so much wildlife in the pitch-dark night.

   _____

13. Uncle Bob, a war veteran, is buried in the Tomb of the Unknowns.

   _____

14. Because of the empty roads, we could coast the last two miles uphill.

   _____

15. "Let me know when you fall asleep," ordered Madeline.

   _____

King of the Mountain!

When the kids were young, there was no game as blood-pumping, as wholly invigorating, as drop-what-you're-doing-and-come-ing as King of the Mountain. To play the game, a hill was required. The mound might be a pile of snow, a dune of sand, a few bales of straw, or even a picnic table. It could be played with two or more players. When a host of players participated, they might choose to split into two teams. Even so, anarchy usually reigned and one's friends and foes might ally to gang up on the king.

You see, one player would dash up the hillock, pose menacingly at the top, and claim, "King of the Mountain!" This challenge demanded an immediate response from all others. If they failed to attack the self-appointed king, they were wimps. Chumps. The scum of the earth. Their duty, their personal honor, required them to attack the king and depose him from the hill. Attackers would pull, push, or tackle to dethrone the king. Then, whoever next reached the lofty heights would reclaim, "King of the Mountain!" And the game would start anew.

School teachers frowned on the game. And for good reason. Bloody noses, arguing combatants, torn clothing, and broken spectacles resulted in phone calls from concerned parents and, consequently, a new Thou Shalt Not . . . rule in the school playground rules book. No, school was no place for this sport.

So the kids played King of the Mountain after school hours on other turf. No supervision. Parents who strongly opposed this play kept their reluctant offspring away. Most parents averted their eyes, crossed their fingers, and prayed for swift healing for whatever injuries would surely occur. Pretty cool. Pretty naive, too.

Injuries did happen. A small sixth grader broke both arms when two attackers crushed him from opposite sides. Another child required stitches when his chin proved softer than his neighbor's skull. A youthful attacker, missing his target, slid over a snow mound hill and skidded into the path of a fast-approaching county snowplow. Only because a fellow player grabbed him by the collar and yanked him into a ditch was a catastrophe avoided. The near-victim was so shaken by this brush with death that he remained in bed for a week.

Another memorable game was played in a barnyard on a pile of soiled hay. In the course of play, the top layer of hay was scuffed and kicked aside, laying bare a goodly patch of pungent, steaming, warm manure, ripe for harvest. A zealous fourth-grade player, screaming a sanguine, curdling oath, charged up the hill, slipped, and plunked down into the freshly-opened pile hands first. His hands, forearms, and elbows disappeared deep into the rich brown-and-yellow mound.

When he was able to pull free, the zealot howled a different tune. Not from ancient Viking frenzy. No. From helpless, childlike anguish and despair. His eyes were popping, his mouth quivering with the onset of tears. His whole being aching to plug closed his nostrils but powerless with digits the center of his olfactoreal malaise. What a picture for the others!

There was no game as blood-pumping, as wholly invigorating, as drop-what-you're-doing-and-come-ing as King of the Mountain. When you're a kid.

And young.

1. What is the intent of this article? _____

_____

2. If you lived with these kids, what would you like about their play?

_____

3. Using headline titles, name the four detailed sufferings in this article.

    a. _____   c. _____

    b. _____   d. _____

4. What is olfactoreal malaise?

_____

5. Choose one to write about on another sheet of paper:
        a list of 10 rules for school ground behavior
        a list of 10 suggestions for parents whose kids play rough sports
        a 50+ word description of a game you know which is similarly rough

6. Match these:
    _____ a. lofty   d. madness
    _____ b. pose   e. very high
    _____ c. frenzy   f. stance

Name _____

You're Never Alone

Manuel was happy to discover that he shared classes with 12 of his friends. But, absent-minded as he is, Manuel needs a diagram to keep track of who's where in his world. Place his friends' names in the proper places in the Venn diagram below.

Name	Band	Physics	Journalism
Arthur	x		x
Brianne		x	
Carrie	x	x	
Dante	x	x	x
Eduard	x		x
Fiona	x	x	x
Gerrit		x	x
Hani	x	x	
Ignacio			x
Jerry	x	x	x
Klaus	x		
Lydia		x	x

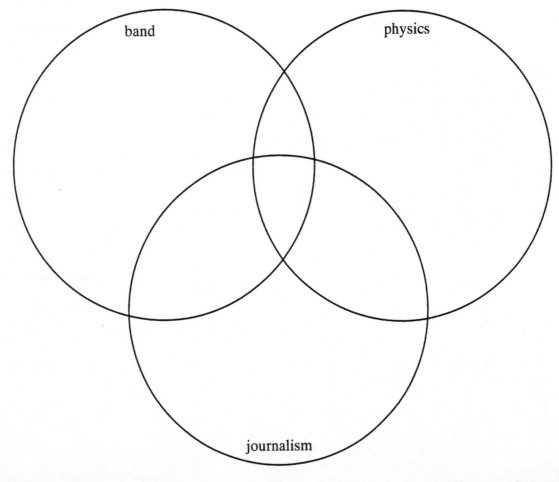

Going to the Hoops

The awesome Anchorage All-Stars, a talented coed basketball team of middle school athletes, whipped their opponents, the Wombats, by 53 points last night. It was not surprising, though. The All-Stars have not lost a game all season. Read their stats, calculate their totals, and answer the questions below as asked by Sports Reporter Madd Leep.

Quarters

Name	1	2	3	4	Total
Layne	4-2*	2-0	3-0	4-3	___
Shane	0-0	1-0	1-1	2-0	___
Jane	0-0	0-1	2-0	1-2	___
Payne	2-0	3-2	1-0	1-2	___
Wayne	6-1	4-0	2-2	2-3	___
Zane	0-2	1-2	1-2	3-1	___
Tippi	3-0	0-0	0-0	2-2	___
Totals	___	___	___	___	___

1. Hey, Coach, who scored the most free throws? _____

2. . . . And how many free throws was that? _____

3. I heard someone scored exactly 18 points? Who? _____

4. Tippi played two quarters because of fouls. Which two? _____

5. Uh, huh. And what was your team's final score? _____

6. Their opponent outscored them by four points in the quarter your All-Stars scored 27 points. Which quarter was this? _____

7. . . . Ah, how many points did the Wombats score that quarter? _____

8. Which two players ended the game with equal scores? _____

9. Wayne was super hot, shooting a mean 67% from the field. How many shots did he take? _____

10. Zane shot 87.5% from the free throw line. How many misses did he have? _____

11. Your two starting guards' scores total 35 points. Who were these sizzling hot players? _____

12. In which quarter did your team score the most points?

*The first number denotes field goals scored, each worth two points. The second number denotes free throws scored, each worth one point.

Hello, and Good Evening

During Choose a Profession Week, Francesca Fontaine bummed around with her uncle, Brett Breathmint, the local television personality. For three days she wrote and reported on the air on three different topics. Here they are.

1. You think it's hot now! Well, I'm telling you it's going to be a downright scorcher the next couple of days. According to Ernest Kalinski, our chief regional meteorologist, cool relief won't be in sight until the middle of next week. Bring out the electrical fans and air conditioners. Nighttime temperatures are expected to drop only to the mid 80s. Today was the fourth day of 100+ degree heat. And the rain promised earlier today? Oops! Put those umbrellas away. This reporter was reading off the wrong chart. That's it for the weather. Back to you, Uncle Brett.

2. Funeral services will be held tomorrow, the twenty-second, for Ermella Beckinkaul, a longtime member of the local Humane Society. Many of us have fond memories of Ermella, who was a friend to creatures. When a vicious chickadee recently cornered Timmy Naidoo's adorable, harmless cobra, it was Ermella who clubbed the dirty bird and threw it into her compost pile. Her sensitive care for the less fortunate was always readily apparent. Her nephew Bob remembers how she reacted when her puppies were frightened by a neighbor's wandering tabby. "Why, Aunt Ermella, she done took that feline by the tail and flung her into a wild raspberry patch," he recalls. On Saturday, Ms. Beckinkaul passed away peacefully while resting in her rocking chair. In lieu of flowers, family members ask that donations be made to the Dog-Gone-It Biscuit Company.

3. Once again Pokey Palmer slams her Wabash Wildcats to victory with a two-out, bases-loaded three-bagger in the ninth inning of their contest against the neighboring Bridgeport Bunions. The 5'10" first base all-stater scored thrice and hit safely four times in this heavy-handed slugfest which concluded with the score 11–9. Bunions' assistant coach remarked, "With her power, Palmer can play pro ball anytime." Thelma Throwhart pitched the Wildcats to victory. Sabrina Southpaugh suffered the heart-breaking loss.

Write phrases which identify these five people.

1. Ermella Beckincaul   _____
2. Ernest Kalinski   _____
3. Sabrina Southpaugh   _____
4. Timmy Naidoo   _____
5. Pokey Palmer   _____

Circle the subjects of Francesca's three television reports.

Report 1

         weather   sports   national news   advertising   deaths

Report 2

         weather   sports   national news   advertising   deaths

Report 3

         weather   sports   national news   advertising   deaths

Write the word from each article whose definition is listed here.

Report 1

    extremely hot day   _____

    weather scientist   _____

    lessen   _____

Report 2

    feline   _____

    tender   _____

    contributions   _____

    place, stead   _____

Report 3

    three times   _____

    competition, game   _____

    heavy-hitting match   _____

Extra: On a separate sheet of paper, write a report of local news using this information.
Who: Paddy Klein; What: lost her "Hansen" designer lunch pack; When: Thursday morning;
Where: field trip to local pet store.

I Think I'll Be a . . . .

1. □ □ □ W □ □ □ □
2. □ □ H □ □ □ □
3. □ □ E □ □
4. □ □ □ □ N □ □
5. □ □ I □ □ □
6. □ □ G □ □
7. □ □ R □
8. □ □ O □ □ □ □
9. □ □ W □ □ □
10. □ □ U □
11. □ □ P □ □ □ □ □ □
12. □ □ I □ □ □
13. □ □ W □ □ □
14. □ □ □ I □ □
15. □ □ L □ □ □ □ □
16. □ □ □ □ L □ □ □
17. □ □ B □ □ □ □ □ □
18. □ □ E

Definitions:

1. builds boats
2. designs buildings
3. explores underwater
4. trades goods
5. makes suits
6. directs others at work
7. tills the soil
8. works with numbers
9. does the backstroke
10. plays percussion instruments
11. takes pictures
12. constructs homes
13. advocates at a trial
14. fixes teeth
15. flies a plane
16. predicts the weather
17. styles and cuts hair
18. teaches classes

Trepidation

Circle the word which best completes each sentence.

1. Kevin slowly picked up his _____ to play the Chopin nocturne.

   toothpick   clarinet   piano

2. With fearful trepidation he lifted the mouthpiece to his _____.

   ears   chest   lips

3. Out of the bell of his reed instrument came a _____ squawk.

   horrendous   peaceful   loving

4. Mrs. Dee Canon abruptly lowered her _____.

   button   shoe   baton

5. "Who so shockingly _____ in a goose from his or her barnyard?" she queried.

   brought   danced   cooked

6. Feeling so _____ he could have hidden under his chair, Kevin raised his hand.

   daring   awful   sleepy

7. Forty-two pairs of eyes turned to stare at the _____-red face of this would-be Benny Goodman.

   potato   beet   celery

8. Mrs. Canon, noting Kevin's chagrin, calmly regained the attention of her _____.

   ears   clarinet   class

9. "Who can tell me the last time they didn't make a rude sound with a _____ instrument?" she began.

   scientific   musical   electronic

10. "Oh, " entered Sean _____, "I remember that four months ago Sunday I didn't make a mistake."

    understandingly   madly   cryptically

11. "And _____ was that?" asked Mrs. Canon, amused by Sean's wisdom.

    who   what   why

12. "Well, you know, we didn't get our instruments until the next _____," replied Sean.

    Christmas   pizza   Monday

13. Mrs. Canon looked at every band member who _____ and nodded their heads.

    hollered   smiled   marched

14. "Kevin," she said softly, "you're doing fine. My goodness! I _____ on my trumpet for two years solid. Just ask my mother."

    squealed   stepped   played

15. Kevin almost smiled, though he kept his head _____.

    nodding   askew   lowered

16. Raising her baton once more, Mrs. Canon returned to the nocturne, and the _____ played on.

    game   band   toys

Smiling

Henry Wadsworth Wordsmith was in a dreadful pickle. And this was peculiar because Henry was a cautious, superbly organized planner.

A week ago Shanda Lira had called him. Shanda, a kind classmate, wondered if Henry would be willing to care for Mitzi, her dog. Well, Henry didn't know. His mom kept a neat house and was allergic to cats. Mitzi's a dog, Shanda said. Yes, well, Henry had had a miserable experience with a pet years ago. Don't think of Mitzi as a pet. Think of her as a little sister, suggested Shanda.

Deep inside, Henry wanted a pet. One to hold. One to care for. What did she look like? Mitzi's an alert, black-and-white rat terrier. She has ears as big as her face and she flits around like a nervous ballerina. But she's gentle and loves to snuggle. Okay, Henry agreed. Perhaps her debasing detriments will not outweigh her more alluring attributes. Whatever, Shanda replied.

That was last week. Yesterday evening Shanda called to say she was bringing Mitzi right over. Henry, unable to mask his enthusiasm, dashed outside to await the arrival. He wore his gray Mr. Rogers sweater, combed his immaculately styled hair, and checked his shoes for scuff marks. When Shanda and Mitzi hopped out of the car, Henry set his sweater aside and came over. Mitzi scampered over, pawed on Henry's legs, and smiled up at him. Well, it looked like a smile!

"My goodness! She likes me!" cried an amazed Henry.

"Oh, yeah. She loves most everyone," explained Shanda. "Here's her junk." Shanda handed over dog dishes, food, cage, leash, cushion, and puppy toys. After giving a few instructions, Shanda rode off with her father.

"Well, Mitzi, I imagine you're hungry," began Henry nervously. He and the dog entered the house where they made their way to the kitchen. Henry set out a mat, placed the water and food dishes on it, measured out the water and food with a measuring cup, and hovered over the canine creature while it chowed down as if it were at home. When Henry sat down on the sofa in the den, Mitzi trotted over and leaped into his lap.

Henry was in heaven. He never thought holding a warm animal could be so fulfilling. After a few minutes of quiet repose, Henry softly said, "Would you like a walk?" From the shaking creature's enthusiasm, the boy surmised that she would. So Henry grabbed Mitzi's leash, and the two were off for a lengthy and invigorating stroll.

But where to let Mitzi sleep? Mother would never let the cage be placed in the den or living room. And Henry refused to have it set in the garage. Finally they compromised, and the cage was put in the kitchen. When Henry said good night to Mitzi, closed the cage door, and turned off the lights, Mitzi let out a howl. Henry cringed as he climbed the stairs to his room. The howl continued. Sheet and blankets over his head, Henry still heard the cry. And Mother's complaint at the door, "Henry, that beast is in **your** charge. Do something!" was no help.

He entered the kitchen, opened the cage door, scooped up the whimpering Mitzi, and quietly, stealthily brought the quavering animal to his room. Mother would not approve.

In the morning Mitzi woke Henry with a face washing. Henry rubbed his eyes and carried Mitzi downstairs. He opened the back door and said, "Okay girl. Do your thing. I'll return in a second."

But after pouring a measured portion of dog food and bringing it to the back door, Henry saw no Mitzi.

"Hey, girl. Where are you? Come here, Mitzi," he called. Nothing. Henry set the bowl down. He dashed down the steps.

"Over here, Mitzi. It's me, Henry!" Nothing. Henry scanned the yard. He walked through the garden. He looked behind shrubs. He circled to the front yard. He looked up and down the boulevard. No Mitzi.

"Oh, no! I lost her!" he whispered. Henry went to the neighbors. He knocked on doors. He walked through yards. He even checked the street gutters. All to no avail. Could someone have stolen her?

After an hour of searching, Henry returned home. He sat on the back porch and picked up Mitzi's food dish. Unconsciously, he picked up nuggets and dropped them back into the dish. And then . . . .

Henry heard a playful growl from beneath the porch steps. There, on Henry's soiled and now torn sweater lay Mitzi. She was shredding the sweater with her teeth. She looked up, panting. And smiling, Henry thought.

"Hey, Mitzi. Are you alright?" Mitzi danced out and leaped into Henry's lap once more.

Put these events in order.

1. _____ Mitzi eats her food   _____ Mitzi licks Henry's face   _____ Henry agrees to dog sit

   _____ Mother complains to Henry   _____ Henry hears a growl

   _____ Mitzi first leaps into Henry's lap

2. _____ Henry loses Mitzi   _____ Mitzi paws Henry's legs

   _____ Henry awaits the arrival   _____ Mitzi comes from under the porch

   _____ Shanda leaves   _____ Henry knocks on neighbors' doors

Give these details.

3. Main Characters _____   _____

   _____   _____

4. Time _____

5. Place _____

6. Story's Problem _____

   _____

7. Do you find Henry appealing or unappealing? Give one reason.

   _____

Got a Match, Bud?

Circle the synonym of each of the highlighted words below. The circled words, when put in their numbered spaces, will form sentences.

1. **wing**	arm	fly	feather	cable	(3)
2. **oceans**	continents	lakes	vistas	seas	(6)
3. **fowls**	pteranodons	rabbits	birds	bones	(1)
4. **spacious**	vast	burgeon	absent	mouthful	(5)
5. **beyond**	toward	against	across	near	(4)
6. **noiselessly**	silently	surely	amusingly	slowly	(2)

_____ _____ _____ _____ _____ _____
  (1)   (2)   (3)   (4)   (5)   (6)

1. **ascended**	mastered	shuffled	climbed	twisted	(4)
2. **compliant**	taciturn	shy	obsolete	obedient	(2)
3. **ancient**	hardened	transient	absolute	old	(6)
4. **warily**	merely	cautiously	extreme	tiredly	(1)
5. **grating**	creaky	charming	boxing	stony	(5)
6. **benches**	stiles	spines	goals	pews	(7)
7. **juveniles**	renegades	children	parrots	villains	(3)

_____ _____ _____ _____ _____ _____ _____
  (1)   (2)   (3)   (4)   (5)   (6)   (7)

1. **brawny**	dour	clean	stout	smart	(2)
2. **determinedly**	thoughtfully	sanely	resolutely	mutely	(7)
3. **toted**	hauled	gave	wrote	painted	(4)
4. **cases**	shelves	levers	tops	cartons	(6)
5. **roustabouts**	angels	chickens	grievances	laborers	(3)
6. **a gross**	20	money	short	144	(1)
7. **icebox**	frigid	refrigerator	cubic	storage	(5)

_____ _____ _____ _____ _____ _____ _____
  (1)   (2)   (3)   (4)   (5)   (6)   (7)

Cul-de-sac Heaven

Donnie and three classmates, Erin, Fabia, and Glen, love outdoor sports. You can find them playing in the streets by their houses. Their homes are on four different streets: Nob, Oakleaf, Pinto, and Quincy. Each street is a cul-de-sac. Each of the four youths has a favorite sport—road croquet, skateboarding, speedball, and street hockey. And their last names obviously are Howard, Ignatius, Jasperse, and Kulak. Please match the kids to their surnames, streets, and favorite games. Use the grid below to help you to make your decisions.

	Howard	Ignatius	Jasperse	Kulak	Nob	Oakleaf	Pinto	Quincy	Rd croq	Skatebd	Spdball	Str hock
Donnie												
Erin												
Fabia												
Glen												
Road croquet												
Skateboarding												
Speedball												
Street hockey												
Nob												
Oakleaf												
Pinto												
Quincy												

Clues:
1. The speedball player has a first name that is two letters longer than the Howard child's.

2. Glen plays road croquet like a pro. He doesn't live on Oakleaf.

3. Ignatius's first name is listed before Kulak's. Ignatius lives on Quincy. Kulak just adores street hockey.

4. Donnie's house is on Pinto.

	First Name	Last Name	Street	Game
1.	_____	_____	_____	_____
2.	_____	_____	_____	_____
3.	_____	_____	_____	_____
4.	_____	_____	_____	_____

48

In the Classifieds

As Kyesha glanced through the classified section of the newspaper last night, she came upon some rather peculiar ads. Here are the ads and Kyesha's comments. Match them if you can!

_____ 1. **Chevy 1984 Cavalier:** has all 4 tires. runs. may need work. you must haul it away yourself. $500 or best offer. call Clutch at XXX-XXXX.

_____ 2. **Tired of sitting** around the house doing nothing? Well, we are looking for people who wish to earn money without leaving home. You don't even need to talk to anyone! The position calls for the stuffing of envelopes. Ask for Stu at XXX-XXXX.

_____ 3. **Wanted:** a cool CD player that can play a really good cool sound. Call Duke the Cool Man at XXX-XXXX.

_____ 4. **Deanie Dollies:** like-new dolls include Ducky Down, Rhino Rex, Koala Kate, Antsy Andy, and Wiener Von Schnitzelhund. Each $14. A real bargain. Won't last long! Call Casey at XXX-XXXX.

_____ 5. **Services:** I will sing for your wedding party. I know "Clementine," "I Love You Truly," "Killing Me Softly," and "Loving You." Wages negotiable. Call Kenny at XXX-XXXX.

_____ 6. **Wanted:** somebody to walk my dog. no references needed. choose your days to take my mutt. any age person may apply. See Lucky at XXX-XXXX.

_____ 7. **Ponys' four sail:** we gots a hoarse wo had to coalts! theys reddy four a gud home. call me att XXX-XXXX.

_____ 8. **Lost:** my kitty. She is yellow and fluffy. And she has a collar and it has a name tag. Her name is Peaches and I want her back right now. Please find her. XXX-XXXX

_____ 9. **We are searching** for an extremely intelligent, mathematically gifted adult in the early 20s. Applicant must be a member of Mensa and a graduate of M.I.T. Call Shondelle at XXX-XXXX.

_____10. **For Sale:** Prize international coin collection. Wood sculptures from Cameroon, Ghana, Belize, Japan, and Switzerland. Call XXX-XXXX and ask for Simone.

a. Oh, help! We'll take anyone!

b. Likely he's got a tin ear.

c. Here's a spot for a recluse.

d. Well, maybe the telephone number is correct at least.

e. Duh, does he know any more adjectives?

f. Oh, ho! We've got a world traveller here.

g. This one's not for your average Joe.

h. Not necessarily the most reliable way to go.

i. Okay. Keep your eyes peeled and help the little kid.

j. Good gravy! You could start your own zoo!

Name _____

Plus One

Directions: Add one letter to each of the words below to create the word whose definition you read on the right.

	Word	Letter	New Word	definition
1.	veips	____	_____	bone of lower abdomen
2.	rich	____	_____	a moveable seat with legs and back
3.	veer	____	_____	at no time
4.	think	____	_____	a particular chess piece
5.	cheer	____	_____	a card game
6.	burn	____	_____	of the city
7.	hour	____	_____	rugged, not smooth
8.	stay	____	_____	bread-making fungus
9.	tail	____	_____	essential
10.	chug	____	_____	a sudden vocal expulsion of breath
11.	roan	____	_____	oakseed
12.	rip	____	_____	a couple
13.	purse	____	_____	magnificent
14.	slem	____	_____	stubborn beasts
15.	scout	____	_____	insect
16.	draw	____	_____	a prize
17.	twine	____	_____	cold season
18.	are	____	_____	365 days
19.	rite	____	_____	attempted
20.	rips	____	_____	steeple
21.	teul	____	_____	a woodwind instrument
22.	doing	____	_____	deep violet
23.	gas	____	_____	flaw; complication
24.	tcred	____	_____	straightforward
25.	tear	____	_____	delicacy; candy
26.	vane	____	_____	simple; unsophisticated
27.	some	____	_____	elk-like deer
28.	dour	____	_____	spherical
29.	won	____	_____	frozen precipitation

The vertical letters spell _____.

Get the Picture

1. Draw a one-story house approximately 2" tall in the center of the frame.
2. Place an open porch on the left side of the house.
3. In the front yard (below the house) show 2 children kicking a soccer ball.
4. Beyond the house and on the right place a large tree with a tire swing hanging from a branch.
5. Place a car on the street in front of the house.
6. Show a sidewalk along the street. Create a walkway leading from the sidewalk to the house's front door.
7. Put shutters on the house's two windows.
8. Draw a garden beyond the house complete with scarecrow. Perch two large crows on the scarecrow.
9. Set a row of flowers on the right side of the front door. Place a bush to the left of the door.
10. The house number is equivalent to (95 divided by 5) + 200. Write the number above the door.
11. Place a picket fence along the rear of the backyard (top of frame). A child stares at us from over the fence.
12. Hang wind chimes from the porch.

Inspiration

Mrs. Candy Gramme, the sixth grade English teacher, assigned her class to write a poem. "Write about something you like. Perhaps this beautiful day. Perhaps a sport you enjoy playing or watching. Perhaps a person you admire or adore."

"Oh, boy!" moaned a despondent Madeline. She didn't have a clue what to choose for a poetry topic. Sitting glumly at the dining room table that evening, unable to focus on a central theme, Madeline became distracted by her baby sister.

"Hey, you little squirt! You're my inspiration!" she laughed. And away she wrote.

When Betsy first did grace us with her charm,
I promised Mom I'd keep her from all harm.
I'd hold her tightly, rocking her at night
To scare away the goblins that would fright.

Then came those diapers, noxious with their smell.
Warm baby food ensmearing face as well
As floor, wall, me! "This babe's a creepy snake
Of SIN!" I cried. "She's keeping me awake!"

My days are changed. Her naps preempt all mine.
I cringe to hear her noisy fussy whine.
Her little burp smells linger on my clothes.
My chats with Mom are less than I'd have chose.

Yet anger flees. My heart cries all a'thrill
When in my arms she nestles, cuddly still.

Questions:

1. What is Madeline's assignment? _____

2. Why can't she begin it immediately? _____

3. What does she choose as her topic? _____

4. What does she appear to like most about her sister?_____

5. What are four things she dislikes about her sister? _____

_____

_____

6. What promise did she make her mother? _____

   What is noble about this promise? _____

7. What does *noxious* mean? _____

8. What does *preempt* mean?_____

9. What two words are meant to rhyme but do not? _____

10. How many syllables does each line contain? _____

11. What might the poem's message be? _____

_____

12. Be a rhyme maker. Finish these couplets.
    A noisy child walked up to me . . . .

_____

If cows could bark and dogs could moo,

_____

What I like most about a friend . . . .

_____

When Cousin Corrie comes to town . . . .

_____

Here or to Go?

Shanda, Bob, and Wes stopped at the local McKings Burger Hut following the middle school basketball games last Wednesday. Complete these money problems. Oh, tax is included in the price.

1. Shanda ordered a large sprite for $1.49, a 69-cent fries, and a Chicken Lickin' Sandwich for $1.34. She handed the cashier a five dollar bill. How much change would she receive?

   _____

2. Bob ordered the Crazy Crispy Meal for $3.11, the Boy! Burger for $4.22, and a tossed salad for 98 cents. He handed the cashier a $10 bill. The teller gave him all coins for his change. What change might he have received?

   Q_____ D_____ N_____ P_____

3. Wes also ordered the Boy! Burger. He ordered a chocolate shake for $2.29. Then he remembered he had only $3 in his pocket. How much must he borrow from Shanda and Bob?

   _____

4. While they were seated, the store manager announced that all "second round" orders were at half price if sales receipts were shown. Bob, ever hungry, took Wes, Shanda's, and his receipts and reordered all (for himself, of course). How much did he pay?

   _____

5. Bob makes $1.50 an hour walking his neighbor's dachshunds and his aunt's whippet. How many hours must he work to cover his costs for Wednesday? _____

6. Under the table of their booth Wes found 47 cents. He paid off this amount of his debt to his friends. Now how much does he owe?

   _____

In the Still of the Night

Shaking like a leaf, Kyesha slipped softly out of her sleeping bag. Quietly, stealthily, she slid over to the tent fly. As soon as she stood up outside her tent, she tore down the narrow path to the twins' tent.

"Bianca! Tonya! Wake up!" she hissed. "Let me in. It's Kyesha!"

As fast as two bleary-eyed, half-asleep kids can, Bianca and Tonya obliged. So, within a minute the three were seated cross-legged in the cramped little pup tent.

"What's up, Kye? You act like you've seen Big Foot," giggled Bianca.

Kyesha shuddered and shook. Unable to salve the emotional strain within her, she broke into tears. Sensing that their friend was serious, both Tonya and Bianca scooted over to comfort their weeping friend between them.

"Hey. Come on. Tell us, Kyesha. What is it?" began Bianca.

"And where's Wanda?" continued Tonya.

"That's just *it!*" wailed Kyesha.

Four girls had made this trek into the state forest. They'd done this every summer since they were ten. All were hardy, outdoor kids. They'd hiked five miles with all their gear just the day before. Camping in the wild was child's play.

Kyesha continued. "She's missing. I just woke up a few minutes ago and her sleeping bag was empty . . . and she was gone. I felt around in the dark and touched something sticky. I thinks it's . . . it's . . . blood all over her pillow and sleeping bag! Something awful's happened!"

"Oh, man! Now you're scaring me," wailed Bianca a little too loudly.

"Shh! We gotta keep quiet. Whatever got Wanda may be around yet," warned Kye.

"We-we-well, wha-what do we do?" stammered Tonya, flapping her hands and stomping her feet.

Outside the tent they heard the sound of something thrashing about in the bushes. It was large. It was violent. The three girls looked at one another. Tonya picked up a hatchet. Bianca grabbed a small shovel. Kyesha wielded a foot-long flashlight.

"One . . . Two . . . Three!"

Howling like banshees, the three campers-turned-warriors poured out of the tent. They roared as they clamored into the woods in the direction of the thrashing sound.

"We've got you, you . . . you . . . beast!" spat Tonya.

*"Tonya? Bianca? Kye? Is that you?"

It was Wanda.

Her eyeglasses lost, her face a royal mess, the fourth member of the camping quartet stumbled toward them. Wanda had always struggled with somnambulant behavior. In her sleep she had opened a jar of raspberry jam. Ate some. Spilled gobs. Woke up a bit embarrassed. So she left the tent to wash off in the river about a quarter mile away. On her return, she dropped her glasses. Probably not broken. Sure to find them in the morning. Kinda funny really.

Yeah! Kinda funny! thought Kyesha. Better not be any of that jam on my sleeping bag!

1. Who are the characters? _____
   _____
   Where does this story take place? _____
   _____
   When is this happening? _____
   _____
   What is the problem?_____
   _____

2. Number these occurrences in order. _____ Kyesha notices blood _____The girls charge the thrashing sound. _____ Kyesha leaves her tent. _____ The three girls hear a sound. _____ Wanda is found. _____ Wanda leaves the tent.

3. What might have served the author's purpose better than raspberry jam? _____

4. What if this story had a different ending? Create your own ending starting from the * sign. You may use another sheet of paper.

I've Got a Secret

Identify each creature described below, using names from the Word Bank.

1. I fly in the evening to catch insects. I have large ears unlike birds. Oh, I have hair, too.

   _____

2. I am a weaver. By my art I capture my food. I'll bite my victim to inject it with poison so it's paralyzed. And I'll eat my food when I'm good and ready. Or I'll let my children eat it.

   _____

3. I love to swim, but I fly very well, too. My feathers keep me warm all my waddling days.

   _____

4. Most of us fly at night. We are attracted to light. We have feathery antennae and our young sit around in cocoons.

   _____

5. I have smooth, moist skin and live both on land and in water. My young have tails and must stay in water. I love insects. Humans seem to think I love lily pads.

   _____

6. My babies cling to me as I search for food. I'm hairy, but I do have a smooth, hairless tail. Some folks say I fool my enemies by faking my death.

   _____

7. I nibble greens. My wild cousins blend well with their surroundings but I'm white. I'm hairy. I walk . . . well, I bound really. And I live in a burrow.

   _____

8. I am a hard worker. I have six legs and two antennae. I use my mouth to carry loads, and I can carry a lot for my size. A few of my family fly but most of our large colony are wingless.

   _____

9. When I fly, my wings beat so fast that people can hardly see them. I'm larger than a bumblebee but have only two wings. I can fly backwards.

   _____

10. I flutter and fly in the sunshine. I'll land on milkweeds with all six legs and lay my eggs.

    _____

11. My sense of smell depends on my tongue. I'm scaly, not slimy! I'll swallow rodents whole and let my body digest them. I slither quickly through the grass. I shed my skin as I outgrow it.

    _____

12. It's no joke. My teeth are razor sharp, and I will attack other swimming critters. I've even chomped on birds that land on the water. I'm not fussy, just hungry!

    _____

Word Bank			
ant	bat	blue racer	spider
moth	pike	opossum	
rabbit	monarch	butterfly	
hummingbird	duck	frog	

Guilt

He shambled off to his bedroom, found a sheet of school paper, and turned it over to its bleak bare back side. Grabbed his Valentine's Day pencil and plunked down on the hardwood floor under his bed.

There he wrote.

Dear Mama,
I love you but I am sorry. I broked your favrit dish. You know the one Daddy got you and you cried and said YOU just loved it. Well I broked it.

I didn't try to. Really. I was juest playing with Spud and we was chasin around the table and I knock into the table and the dish felt off and broked.

I love you Mama.

And I know that you must hate me. And I am sorry. I will go away and I won't bother you again and maybe you and Daddy can fix the dish with some glue. I tried the white glue but it didn't work too good.

Maybe if you fix the dish you will want me back. I hope so cuz I miss you already and I'm not even gone yet and I love you so and . . . .

He began to cry. Softly. Whimpering like a cocker puppy. With tears rolling down his cheeks like raindrops on a windowpane in a summer downpour. Quietly so as not to draw attention. Muffled to hold all his pain to himself. The young boy slept.

And woke to hear Mama coming in from the garden. Walking to the kitchen to wash her hands.

The child quickly scrawled his hugs and kisses, signed his name Benjie, placed his missive on the teddy bear comforter of his bed, and stepped into his closet. He'd have to leave when the house was quiet, he thought. Maybe midnight. Yeah, it'd be dark then. Right.

So the boy waited and waited. And he had to go to the bathroom because waiting was so hard, but he didn't want Mama to see him. To hate him. So he sat down on the floor in his closet and quietly cried himself to sleep again.

Mama found the shards of glass. Mama found the glue bottle tipped over, still dripping its thick, glossy essence. Dripping to the floor. She guessed. She sighed.

Mama traced the boy's route to his room. To his bed. To his note which she could hardly read through her own tears.

And to the closet where, scooping up her seven-year-old son, she held him like a newborn, cradled in her arms, feeling his tousled, tear-stained head below her cheek. Pulling him to her and carrying him to her favorite rocker. And she held him warm. Held him tight. Held him long past the time he'd wake up and say,

"Oh, Mama, I love you!"

And they'd cry again.

1. What is the boy's crime? _____

2. What is compared to raindrops? _____

3. The author gives two reason why the boy cries quietly. What are they?
   a. _____   b. _____

4. What do you believe Mama's feelings are when she discovers the glass shards? _____
   _____

5. When she finds the note? _____
   _____

6. Using at least three sentences, argue for or against this statement: The boy's feeling of guilt is a healthy response to his mistake._____
   _____
   _____
   _____
   _____

7. What words in the story are synonyms for the following?
   a. note/message   _____
   b. quilt/blanket   _____
   c. dropped/thudded   _____

Food for Thought

In the Word Bank are the names of 32 food items we could ingest. Please sort them into the proper categories below.

Spices	Desserts	Drinks	Grains/Breads
_____	_____	_____	_____
_____	_____	_____	_____
_____	_____	_____	_____
_____	_____	_____	_____
_____	_____	_____	_____
_____	_____	_____	_____
_____	_____	_____	_____
_____	_____	_____	_____

Word Bank

apple dumpling	bagel	barley	cereal	cider	cinnamon	cloves
cobbler	cola	cracker	cumin	curry	eclair	eggnog
fudge	ginger	hot cocoa	juice	malt	milk	nutmeg
oatmeal	paprika	pasta	pepper	wassail	rice	sorbet
strudel	tortilla	truffle	pumpkin pie			

Memorials

Follow the instructions below to name two well-known U.S. memorials.

1. beginning word

   remove the first letter

   change all T's to P's

   reverse the last two letters

   insert an A following the E

   move the 2nd and 3rd letters to the end

   remove all A's

   reverse all letters; add R before E

   insert LUNT following the 1st letter

   change PL to MO

   insert RUSH following 5th letter

BATTLE

_____
_____
_____
_____
_____
_____
_____
_____
_____
_____
_____

2. beginning word

   place a C in the first position

   reverse the last four letters

   change O to R

   change N to P

   insert A in the 1st and 5th position

   reverse the 5th and 6th letters

   remove letters in the odd-numbered positions

   change C to ROB; change G to P

   reverse all letters

   insert LHAR following the 4th letter

TONGUES

_____
_____
_____
_____
_____
_____
_____
_____
_____
_____
_____

The Washington Monument?

Gettysburg?

With the Guys

Read the paragraphs and then answer the questions that follow.

1 When we left the cafeteria this noon, we headed for the gym. It's where we usually hang. Todd and Nick and us guys shoot hoops, or we, ya know, watch the girls walk by, or we just talk. Well, this time we were just jawing a bit, nothing special, ya know. That's when June came up.

Junior LeBlanc is a bit of a loner. He's a nervous kinda guy, always rubbing his arms and legs. Always pushing his glasses back in place. Always on the outs with us kids. Easy to push around. Nick calls him the Lone Ranger, and Nick's right.

"Hey, ya guys. Watcha doin'?" June says.

"Nothin'." That's Todd.

"Shove off, June."

"Yeah, beat it."

2 Junior just hangs by. He waves his arms like some spastic Tweety Bird and rubs both shoulders. Looks away like he's going somewhere, right? But he has no place to go. Not really.

"Hey, you deaf, LeBlanc?" sneers Nick. "Get away, man. You stink!"

Nick muscles over to him, gets his paws on June's chest, and shoves. Junior stumbles a little but doesn't fall. He just pushes up his glasses and eyes Nick nervously.

Some girls giggle. Hangers on. Lookin' for sport like most of us.

No one speaks for Junior. Don't have anyone here that suicidal. We just nod. We're cool.

"Go find Silver, Lone Ranger," says one kid.

"Yeah, giddyup, little doggie," Nick goes.

Junior's got a red face by now. He's always getting that way. He's shakin' like one of those string puppets, ya know? He actually stares at Nick with a kind of scowl. And the kids, we all say, "Oooh!" And then he scratches his hands, and wrinkles his nose, and galumps off toward the classrooms even though we've got another ten minutes, 'least.

"Man, he's easy!"

"Wasted him." That's Todd's comment.

The guys laugh. We get talkin' about other stuff. Just waitin' til class starts up. We're all moanin' the afternoon's work load. Yeah, we're all one happy family.

3 But I don't know. I mean, when I'm with the guys, I laugh with them. I can be just as tight and nasty as the next guy. And they're like my family, ya know?

That's what I tell myself. But it doesn't do it right for me. I feel, oh I don't know, like maybe we shouldn't a' messed with June like that. That pickin' on him brings us down too.

I useta read. Ya know? Stuff about knights and lords and soldiers. Bravery and courage stuff. It was lame, right? But maybe it's more honest than this. Else why do I think this stuff?

1. Mike, the boy who told this story, spoke with a youth counselor who suggested that perhaps June was braver than the others. He asked Mike why this might be. What would you suggest?

   _____

   _____

2. What is the main idea of the first section? _____

   _____

3. Of the second section? _____

   _____

4. Of the third section? _____

   _____

5. Describe the four character groups using these words: *bully, followers, isolated,* and
   thoughtful.

   Mike _____   Nick _____

   gang _____   June _____

6. Mike's counselor suggested that Mike might know what to do to "make it right." What do you
   think would be two possible solutions?

   a. _____

   b. _____

7. Mike spoke of the guys "like my family, ya know?" What does he mean?

   _____

8. When could a "family" like this be unhealthy or negative? _____

   _____

Commonality

Each word in Bank A shares a feature with a word in Bank B. Can you place them with their appropriate features? Then name another word which shares this feature.

Feature	Bank A word	Bank B word	Your word
1. sense organ	ear	nose	
2. inventor			
3. fabric			
4. to be read			
5. city			
6. container			
7. round			
8. direction			
9. thing you blow into			
10. volume marking			
11. nursery rhyme character			
12. musical genre			
13. football position			
14. disease			
15. color			
16. in Washington, D.C.			
17. souvenir			
18. Egyptian structure			
19. body of water			
20. famous singer			
21. Shakespearean character			
22. communication tool			
23. South American country			
24. bird action			

Bank A: balloon, Bo Peep, bottle, Caspian Sea, Colombia, damask, Denver, ear, Edison, Ella Fitzgerald, fuchsia, glide, label, Lady Macbeth, Lincoln Memorial, linebacker, north, piano, postcard, reggae, rotund, rubella, satellite, Sphinx

Bank B: above, amber, Amman, Bolivia, Buddy Holly, basket, Capitol, Carver, forte, jazz, Jill, linen, minaret, Missouri River, nose, novel, novelty mug, Ophelia, receiver, soar, spherical, strep throat, telegraph, tuba

Proverbial Wisdom

Directions: Circle the word which best fits each blank below.

Saving your (1)____ to eat at a later date is not always (2)____. It may not wait as long as you do!

1. land	greed	luck	dessert
2. golden	wise	fair	sure

Many (3)____ may indeed make for light work, but only if they work (4)____.

3. shovels	seas	hands	kitchens
4. together	alone	nearby	silently

"Put your money where your mouth is" may be a (5)____-inflicting proverb; but it sure (6)____ people quiet!

5. plant	gold	wise	germ
6. invests	keeps	shuts	tempts

Go ahead and rollerblade along life's (7)____, but keep those knee pads (8)____ for the bumps along the way.

7. problems	lanes	lamps	deeds
8. ready	quick	dangerous	softly

Music may indeed (9)____ a savage beast . . . at least if the (10)____ has tamed his instrument.

9. shoot	ride	calm	scale
10. lion	trumpet	radio	musician

The saying "A fool and his money are soon (11) ____" should not be discussed when (12)____ allowance off your folks.

11. parted	happy	peaceful	shown
12. sewing	waving	giving	begging

As Uncle Gene (13)____ on his inflatable raft on the (14)____, we knew that some men are islands!

13. flew	fetched	floated	fared
14. dock	lake	sink	house

Hurtling downward into a deep, dark (15)____, Bernard exclaimed, "Why sure! Gotta (16)____ before ya' leap!"

15. mansion	Chevy	chasm	rim
16. look	shave	care	buy

The Hands of Rodin

Read the following paragraphs. Then use the form on the next page to write the facts in outline form.

Three students from the Frank Lloyd Wright School of the Performing Arts recently represented their state in an international exhibit of student art. All three students entered sculptures.

The first, Jean Molière, created an enormous papier mâché structure he calls *The Golden Gargoyle*. Its massive head, of rocklike nature and stoic form, peers down and out as though scrutinizing the mere mortals standing below. This creature is fitted with comic, playful wings much too small to lift his bulky form. The beast appears to wear a long tunic of metal disks, scale-like, almost reptilian, which cover him from shoulder to knee. His feet, oddly enough, are webbed like a platypus.

Cherise de Calderon chose clay as her medium to mold an exquisite form called *The Supper Table*. Calderon's clay form rests on a low, square, thick-legged table textured with a heavy oak-grain surface. Upon this table rest two simple mugs and plates glazed a deep royal blue. Beside each plate is set a knife and fork so silver-like so as to fool the viewer. Clay form breads, cheeses, and various fruits glazed in realistic color are spread upon the table. Finally, placed at the table's center is a rustic, wood-like candlestick holding the only real object, a white wax candle.

The third entry is a marvelous paper creation by Chris Marlowe called *Metropolis 2500*. It is a futuristic cityscape of rounded towers, pointed spires, octahedral and dodecahedral structures, spheres, and prisms of various dimensions. Visually, the form pulls together with ribbon-like highways which swoop and soar through the city plan. Futuristic vehicles for air and land are strategically placed to pique our interest. Opposed to this mass of unadorned white paper sculpting is placed a center of bright green paper work, a landscaped park complete with forests, lakes, fields, and pastures.

The Hands of Rodin
Three Sculptures

Sculpture Medium

I. *The Golden Gargoyle*   -- papier mâché

   A. Massive head

   B. _____

   C. _____

   D. Webbed feet

II. _____   -- clay

   A. _____

   B. Two sets of mugs and plates

   C. _____

   D. Models of bread, fruits, and cheese

   E. _____

III. *Metropolis 2500*   -- _____

   A. _____

   B. _____

   C. Futuristic vehicles for air and land

   D. _____

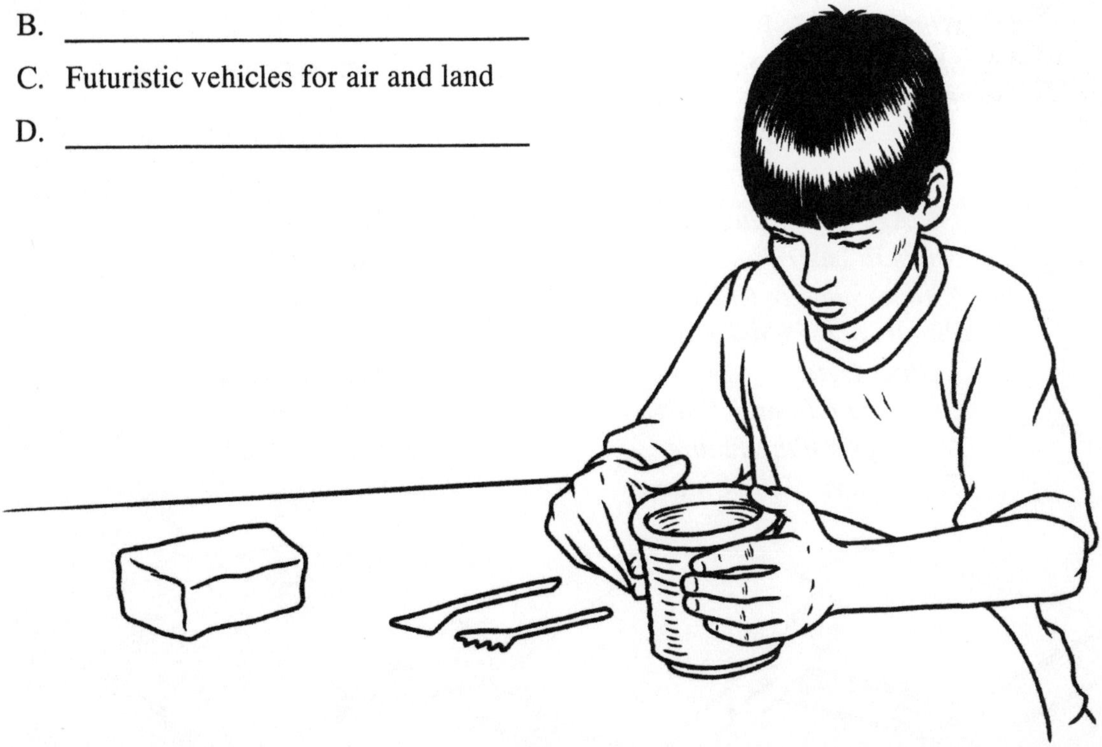

The Writers' Block

Along Hawthorne Street between Hemingway and Alcott live 26 writers. In the past month each has had his or her latest story, article, or book published. Match each writing to its author.

Part 1

_____ 1. *Mighty Fine Food, Ma'am*

_____ 2. *All Those Teeth*

_____ 3. *Percussive Persuasion*

_____ 4. *Desserts from the Orchard*

_____ 5. *Know Yourself*

_____ 6. *Those Laundry Day Blues*

_____ 7. *Buried Treasure*

_____ 8. *Tales of Nightly Terror*

_____ 9. *Lowering Your Cholesterol*

a. Sherry Pye

b. Freddy Katt

c. Howie Doen

d. Barb E. Kew

e. Les S. Gud

f. Phil Theesachs

g. Tim Pani

h. Doug Dieper

i. Barry Kuda

Part 2

_____ 10. *Tribute to the 50s*

_____ 11. *Tub Toys for Tots*

_____ 12. *Silence in the Sahara*

_____ 13. *Breakfast Mania*

_____ 14. *Favorite Bumper Stickers, a Photo Essay*

_____ 15. *A Christmas Cheer*

_____ 16. *Whose Vault Is It?*

_____ 17. *She Sells Sea Shells*

_____ 18. *The Striped Beast*

j. Hammond Eks

k. Reed DeWurtz

l. Rob R. Dukkey

m. Perry Winkle

n. Bobby Sachs

o. Klaus O'Taiger

p. Holly N. Ivie

q. Kent U.B. Stihl

r. Jim Nasticks

Part 3

_____ 19. *The Age of Wearing Down*

_____ 20. *Knots to Last*

_____ 21. *A Tour Guide of Chicago*

_____ 22. *Pitfalls of the Credit Card*

_____ 23. *A Blind Date*

_____ 24. *Choosing a Family Car*

_____ 25. *A Glimpse of the Future*

_____ 26. *The History of the Cinema*

s. Kerrie Kash

t. Mark E. Bijou

u. Peter Aut

v. Willy B. Wright

w. Wendy Seedie

x. T. Leeves

y. Steve Adour

z. C. Dann

What's the Word?

Fill in the blanks with the list words provided.

Part 1

While in New Bristol, Bertie and I bought a newspaper at a (1)_____. As we

(2)_____ the paper, I noticed out of the corner of my eye a young boy

(3)_____ on a nearby park bench. Poor lad! He was fit to be tied! Why, he was on the

(4)_____ of despair. In Bertie's (5)_____ he had a story worthy of the

newspaper we held.

    word list: brink   fidgeting   examined   opinion   kiosk

Part 2

With a (6)_____ heart, the beast entered the stable offered by the human. She knew

well to (7)_____ this two-legged creature. And the (8)_____, pleased to

show kindness to this miraculous beast, could scarcely contain himself. As he forked hay from the

barn (9)_____, he shook his head and clucked his tongue. "To think," he mused, "that

I should be visited by a mythical (10)_____!"

    word list: innkeeper   loft   grateful   unicorn   trust

Part 3

"I am shocked to the (11)_____ of my being! What (12)_____ is this

when you choose to (13)_____ your clothes over our precious antique love seat? That

is no way to (14)_____ yourself to my goodly nature! Be aware that strict attention to

our museum's guidelines is of (15)_____ importance if you wish to retain your post

with us!"

    word list: drape   vital   nonsense   core   endear

Part 4

He awoke from his (16)_____. Snorting, coughing, the young (17)_____

noticed the building's smoke. A (18)_____ of park visitors had lit a fire in the wood

stove in an adjoining room but had forgotten to open the damper. The child (19)_____

for fresh air. How could he (20)_____ such a dusky, soot-filled building? So out he

crept to find lodging elsewhere.

    word list: habituate   quartet   slumber   urchin   yearned

Write Me a Letter

July 26

Dear Mrs. Brewton,

Aloha from the big island! This state is so beautiful! We had the chance to drive fairly close to the volcano again this week. No activity, but that's okay. The sugar cane workers of the area love the weather we've been having lately. That sure looks like hard work to me!

I've gotten to know a few more kids this past week. I'm surprised how many friends I've made in the short time I've been here since school got out in June. By the way, how are things in North Country? Any news from those pesky Americans to your south? And how is the exchange student my parents are hosting this summer? Her name is Rachel, right? I think it's great that someone is using my room while I'm doing the same over here. The Posts, by the way, are a great couple and their kids sure love to tell me everything about the land here. I'll bring back some good tropical specimens to share with you for school.

It's weird to think there's just a couple of years left in high school. Thanks for getting me into this program. I never thought I'd ever get to see those plants and animals you told us about in class last year. I gotta thank my parents, too. I don't think it was easy for them to let their daughter out of their sight for so many weeks.

About every day we kids have a chance to kick the ol' ball around. I'm not playing fullback or goalie as much as I do for our school's team back home. Hey, did you know that these guys didn't know our city was the capital of our province? Many of them never even heard of the CN Tower or the Royal Ontario Museum. So when they found out how much I know about this sport, they went lame. I guess they thought we only played hockey and raced dogsleds or something.

Say, before I forget, how is Fletch doing? Thanks for taking care of him while I'm gone. Dad was kinda worried about that. He said he had no clue how to care for such a critter. Now that Fletch has turned 60, his diet has changed a bit. Let me know what you think of his coloring. It seems to me his green feathers are a bit less glossy than they should be. Although I miss him and he misses me (he does call me "Lady Love," you know), I know he's in good hands. Just don't teach him too many new words. His vocabulary is already greater than that of half the sophomore class!

I can't wait until the twelfth. That's when we fly off to the Land of the Rising Sun. Wow, to think that I'll be flying clear to the other side of the world! Crazy, huh? The Posts are kinda surprised. They thought I'd be more homesick by now. And I would be, but there is so much to see here. And then to top it all off with a flight to visit our sister city in Asia, to see Shinto shrines, Mount Fuji, another culture. I am so excited!

Tell Mom and Dad I love them. Of course I'm writing them again tomorrow, but you know what I mean. The boys here are as shy around me as most guys are back on King Street. Kinda funny. Kids are pretty much the same wherever you go.

I'll see you next fall. Thanks for the birthday card. Never thought you'd remember. Well, I guess I did.

With great appreciation,
Chris

Answer these questions. You must read between the lines to get them all.

1. Where is Chris living this summer? _____

2. How long has Chris been there? _____

3. What is the purpose of the trip? _____

4. Is Chris a boy or a girl? _____

5. How old is Chris? _____

6. What does Mrs. Brewton teach? _____

7. What kind of pet does Chris own? _____

8. Where does Chris go next? _____

9. Where is Chris' home? _____

10. What is Chris' favorite sport? _____

Lay It on the Line

Read the paragraph below, paying attention to the bold-faced phrases. Then write each phrase to match its literal meaning below.

We were having a good time in the school hallway when **out of the clear blue sky** Jana started up. I knew it! She just had to ask me about my trip to Jamaica. Oh shoot, she really had me **over a barrel**. Man! I wanted to **fly the coop**. You see, a couple days before, I had lied about going to Jamaica. Sure, Jana's been there, but not me! It seems I **can't hold a candle to** her when it comes to interesting vacations to brag about.

"Why, Dougie," Jana teased. "What's wrong, honey? **Cat got your tongue?**" She smiled roguishly at me.

Boy, that girl sure **hit the nail on the head** with that question. And then she nagged me all day long.

I warned her to **cool it**. You can't imagine how angry she makes me. Shoot! She didn't listen though. She really had a **one-track mind**. I was a **sitting duck** to her digs and verbal jabs. Then she started bragging about all her trips around the world! And the rest of the class was **all ears** to anything she'd say. **In a nutshell** that girl is and always will be **too big for her britches**.

literal meaning	idiom
1. in a few words	_____
2. is greatly inferior	_____
3. eager to listen	_____
4. calm down	_____
5. thinking oneself is so important	_____
6. unable to defend oneself	_____
7. escape	_____
8. was correct	_____
9. thinks about only one subject	_____
10. helpless; at a disadvantage	_____
11. is there a reason you're silent?	_____
12. without warning	_____

A Far-Off Place

On the planet of Utopia, rain never falls. Of course, hail and snow, the only two precipitation forms known there, are both common and somewhat dangerous. (This is why Utopian meteorology is a highly paid profession.) Fortunately, there are lulls in the Utopian nine-month year when citizens can enjoy the bright Rigelian sun. Read the graph below to answer the questions.

1. Which month has a total precipitation of 9 cm? _____

2. The precipitation *always* melts within 12 hours of its accumulation. During which two months would you expect the most flooding? _____

3. Which is normally greater, hail or snow accumulation? _____

4. During which two months does Utopia have equal snowfalls? _____

5. If Charmain, a tourist agent, enjoys sending people on vacations when there is less than ten cm of precipitation, what months would she choose? _____

6. How much hail is expected in Fern? _____cm

7. Why is the month of Fern unique? _____

8. What is the total yearly snowfall expected on Utopia? _____cm

9. What is the total yearly hail accumulation? _____cm

10. Rate the months from driest to wettest.

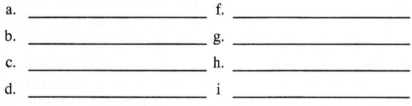

   a. _____   f. _____

   b. _____   g. _____

   c. _____   h. _____

   d. _____   i _____

   e. _____

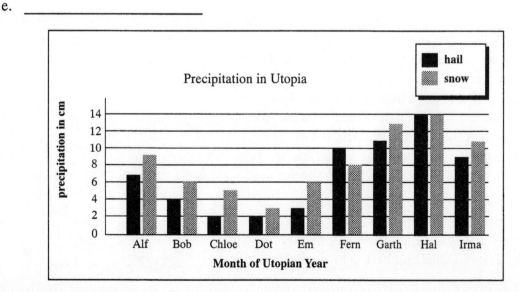

Peppermints

Hannah *lived* in church. Why, she and her family went to church twice every Sunday! And they went to all sorts of prayer meetings, too. Her sister Marty and she went to the Summer Bible School, and Sunday School, and the Tiny Voices, the choir for adolescent members of the congregation. Marty said that Tiny Voices was a stupid name. They weren't babies! Hannah thought it was a funny name. Hannah and her best friend Abby would scream, "Tiny Voices!" Then they'd toddle about like babies in drunken circles across the choir room and gurgle, "Yabba, yabba, yabba, yabba!" in no particular tune for no particular reason as loudly as they could until Miss Frens, their patient and long-suffering choir director, would quiet them down. And Hannah, Marty, Abby, and the others would stop whatever they were doing, walk meekly to Miss Frens, and kneel in a circle at her feet. Kinda like the 12 disciples.

Hanna's family always got to church 15 minutes early. Da liked to sit in a certain pew. So the church saved this pew for Hannah's family. Da said it made church more like home. It was safe. It was comfortable. It was restful.

Hannah always felt safe at church, too. And she tried to feel comfortable even though once she turned five Mama and Da wouldn't let her take her blankey anymore. And church was very restful! Lots of times Hannah even fell asleep.

There was a man in church. An old man. He had bulging pockets in his suit coat. And he had big ears, a lo-o-ong nose, and a warm, wonder-filled smile smack dab in the middle of his face. His pockets were saturated with peppermints. White and pink ones. And after church every Sunday all the kids would flock around this candy shepherd. And every Sunday he would disperse candy until his pockets were empty. Sometimes Hannah got three, four, or even five mints! And she would slowly dissolve them in her mouth all the way home from church. And if she didn't eat them all, that was okay! She could suck on them during the sermon or the long prayer the next Sunday.

One Sunday, the family got to church late. Da couldn't find his keys. Marty's hair needed to be braided. Hannah lost her shoes. So when they got to church, they had to sit in the balcony. Up the squeaky stairs. On the older, firmer, colder wooden pews. Way up yonder. With the late people.

But the worship service began. Everyone stood and sang. And sat down. And stood to sing again. It was then that Hannah felt in her coat pocket and discovered two peppermints! So when everyone sat down, Hannah got out the first candy. It was white. It was sweet. It melted away in her mouth far too quickly. Hannah tried to keep busy. She watched the ceiling. She spied out the tall, narrow, arched windows. She counted the heads of the worshippers below. She followed the minister's gestures as he waved his hands about as though he was shaking hands with the wind.

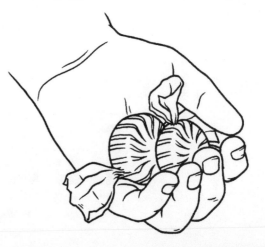

And then she got out her second mint. Oh! It was pink! Pinkies were special. And into her mouth it popped. Right there on her tongue. Right there in the mid . . . Aughk! Awk! The mint had slid back into Hannah's throat. Hannah went bug-eyed. Oh, it hurt. Oh, it was awful. Aughk! Augh! Awk! She croaked. Mama looked at her suspiciously. Da scowled and raised his eyebrow. But then Mama knew Hannah wasn't playing. She sent her with Marty down to the basement. To the bathroom. To the toilet. To spit up the mint.

And she did.

But not until she had croaked a hundred croaks. Not until she cried big, juicy-sweet tears, Not until she covenanted with God that she would never consume another mint in church. And she didn't. For awhile.

1. Use the context of the story and a dictionary if you wish to give the meanings of these words.

   adolescent _____

   *long-suffering*_____

   gesture _____

2. Why does Hannah's family come to church early?

   _____

   _____

3. What does Hannah call the old man with the peppermints? Why?

   _____

   _____

4. Why was the family late this Sunday?

   a. _____   b. _____

   c. _____

5. Why does Hannah croak?

   _____

6. How does she get over her predicament?

   _____

7. Tell about a time you were "sent out" from a room or gathering.

   _____

   _____

   _____

8. Da thought the church was safe. Do you have a special safe place? Where is it? What makes it safe for you?

   _____

   _____

   _____

Fly This Past Me

Each of the rebuses below is the name of a bird. Can you ID these birds?

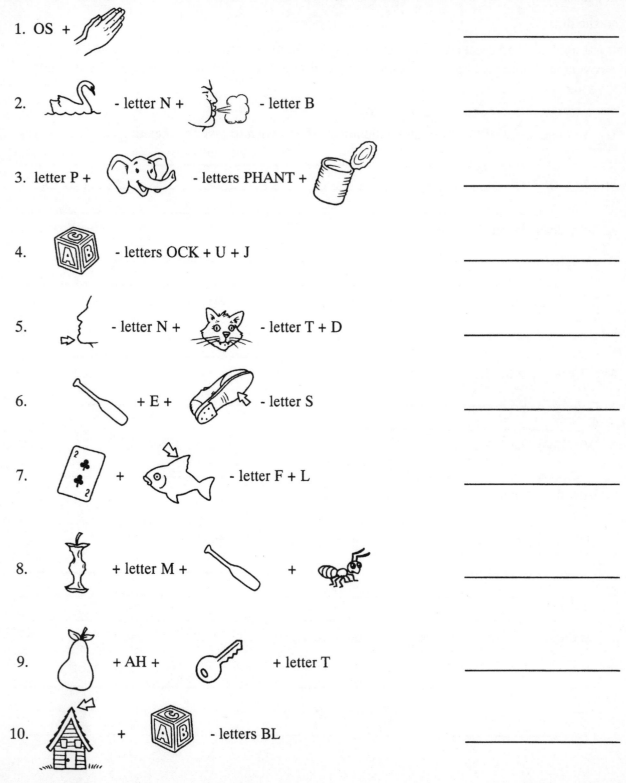

1. OS + 🙏 _____

2. 🦢 - letter N + 💨 - letter B _____

3. letter P + 🐘 - letters PHANT + 🥫 _____

4. [block] - letters OCK + U + J _____

5. 👤 - letter N + 🐱 - letter T + D _____

6. [bat] + E + [shoe] - letter S _____

7. [2 of clubs] + [fish] - letter F + L _____

8. [apple core] + letter M + [bat] + [ant] _____

9. [pear] + AH + [key] + letter T _____

10. [house] + [block] - letters BL _____

Take Your Pic

Place the letter of the correct picture in the blank beside its definition.

_____ 1. a dreidel on a chiffonier

_____ 2. a flounder on gneiss

_____ 3. a submersed dinghy

_____ 4. a bilious bighorn

_____ 5. a mikado with a trident

_____ 6. a doughty doughboy

_____ 7. a gnomen by a kirk

_____ 8. a rueful toreador

Telling Tales

"It's all right, son. Yeah, yeah, calm down. Sure I'll fix it!

"Sorry about that. He's still upset about the break-in, you understand. It'll probably give him nightmares for some time. Scarred for life, you know? Kids these days!

"Yeah, of course we got a good look at her! Wouldn't wonder if she broke into other homes too . . . No, no one else was here that I know of. Just that girl. You want her description again? How many times . . . ? Yeah, alright. Alright already!

"Has the meanest, grumpiest-looking face you ever did see. She was wearing a forest green jacket and expensive running shoes. Eyes were kinda close set. I think they were dark, maybe brown. I don't know! She did have shiny blond hair, almost yellow. And she wore one of those Gilligan sailor hats, you know what I mean?

"I'm guessing she came right in the back door by the kitchen. Grabbed whatever food she wanted from there. Let's see . . . cookies, a coupla apples, apple juice, my son's cereal . . . yeah, it was still out. Like I said, we rushed my wife to the hospital as soon as she got stung by that crazy bee. She's allergic, remember? . . . a coupla slices of bread, toasted it seems, and even a cup of coffee. Greedy little whippersnapper, don't you think?

"How do I know? Well, for one thing there were crumbs all over the kitchen counter. And, and a spanking new loaf of bread was opened and some slices were gone! Okay? Believe me now?

"Well, I don't know. She coulda been in every room of the house for all I know. But she was certainly in the living room. Man, the newspaper was scattered here, there, everywhere. My reading light was on. And this is what's criminal. She had the **audacity** to break my little boy's rocker! That girl had no business setting her fanny down in my son's favorite chair! Shows a total lack of morals, don't you know? I have no idea how to fix that rocker. It's a one-of-a-kind, ya see.

"Oh, you want to hear about us surprising her?

"No, it's not so odd! We're redoing the boy's room. Paint and carpet work mostly. So we moved his bed into our room to escape the paint fumes. You wanna see the room again? Okay.

"Yeah, it's a beauty, huh? My wife likes a soft mattress. I like a firmer mattress so we each get our way with this duo-mattress bed . . . oh, yeah, that prowler was tucked under the covers on my side when we came in . . . No, we weren't extra quiet when we came. Never expected to catch the kid . . . Why, I just pulled back the cover and said, 'Hey, you **varmint,** get outta my bed. This isn't no Holiday Inn!' Well, sir, she opened her eyes, looked at me like I was goin' to eat her up, popped out of that bed like a jack-in-a-box, and high-tailed it down the steps.

"Do I? Why, sure I wanna press charges! That's illegal entry. These two-legged humans think they own the place, don't they?"

1. What story is this? _____

2. Who is telling the story? _____

3. How is it like the original? _____

   _____

   _____

4. We never read the police detective's words. But we can imagine some of her/his questions. Write two of those questions.

   _____

   _____

   _____

   _____

5. What additional damage *might* the intruder have made to the house? _____

   _____

6. Why had the owner's family left the house so quickly? _____

   _____

7. What is meant by the words . . .
   audacity? _____
   varmint? _____

8. What does it mean to be "scarred for life"? _____

   _____

In the Mood

Humans are capable of exhibiting a variety of moods. Match each situation with its mood.

a. domineering   b. generous   c. interested   d. timorous   e. weary

_____ 1. Sixteen hours of babysitting with no sleep! And that baby . . . was she awake again? Ohhh!

_____ 2. Man, was *he* ever going to get this team in shape! Rex, captain of the team, knew he had great ideas!

_____ 3. Terri eavesdropped as her parents discussed what she hoped would be the best vacation of the century.

_____ 4. Required to speak in front of a huge audience, Barry's knees knocked, his face reddened, and his voice croaked.

_____ 5. Stanley willingly let his younger sister have the larger piece of angel food cake.

a. electrified   b. lackadaisical   c. prudent   d. skeptical   e. somber

_____ 6. Well, thought Jon, I suppose I could help Mom with the garbage. But not now. Maybe in a couple of days.

_____ 7. Now! Is my teacher really Mr. Roger's nephew? Naw!

_____ 8. The gang was silent. They had just heard that Danielle's sister had been in a horrid accident.

_____ 9. Another point is scored! The crowd is going wild!

_____ 10. Okay, so the new puppy isn't housebroken yet. Better put some newspaper down on the floor just in case . . . .

a. chagrined   b. disputatious   c. sluggish   d. upbeat   e. whimsical

_____ 11. The ninth grade boys put on flowery hats and sat down at small tables for their dubious tea party.

_____ 12. Penny had been down with the flu for three days. She felt as though she couldn't move!

_____ 13. "Hey, what a great day!" shouted Shakira. "The sky is clear and I feel wonderful!"

_____ 14. Gord looked into the mirror, only to discover that he still had toothpaste on his nose from that morning.

_____ 15. If Wendy were feeling ornery, she would have argued that the sun was blue and the sky was green.

Mm-Mm-Good!

Here are your M words. Well. . . there are 24 words beginning with the letter M hidden in the puzzle. Circle each word and write it next to its definition below. You may need to consult a dictionary.

1. monkey _____
2. waterproof cloak _____
3. wild _____
4. purplish-rose color _____
5. enlarge _____
6. corn _____
7. with evil intent _____
8. poisonous tree snake _____
9. estate _____
10. gourd-like percussion instrument _____
11. weasel-like carnivore _____
12. bullfighting swordsman _____

13. bladed, digging tool _____
14. wedlock _____
15. unleavened bread _____
16. scanty _____
17. very likely _____
18. wander aimlessly _____
19. highly contagious viral disease _____
20. tuneful _____
21. souvenir _____
22. shooting star _____
23. cage for birds of prey ___
24. mix or blend _____

```
M  E  A  S  L  E  S  J  I  O
R  O  Ł  T  E  M  U  H  D  T
M  E  L  O  D  I  O  U  S  N  R  P
A  U  G  Z  M  A  I  Z  E  E  O  A
G  Q  N  T  P  A  C  D  A  M  D  H
N  A  I  A  M  M  I  A  M  E  A  Y
I  C  M  M  M  M  L  M  R  M  T  A
F  A  M  A  M  B  A  M  O  A  A  M
Y  M  A  T  R  I  M  O  N  Y  M  E
H  S  O  T  N  I  K  C  A  M  G  A
E  C  M  O  M  M  F  L  M  K  M  G
W  E  M  C  A  T  N  E  G  A  M  E
   N  K  M  E  A  N  D  E  R  R
   M  A  R  T  E  N  B  M  M  A
```

American Graffiti

Stuck in front of the tube again. Just stuck.

No energy to get off his lazy duff and play ball. No will to get up and do his house chores. Not even enough gumption to raid the fridge for a snack.

Not that the TV had much to offer.

There was that stupid soap about all these lovelorn grownups acting like . . . well, actually acting younger than he felt. There was that weird courtroom drama where adults yelled and screamed at each other. As though they were really angry. Like it was the end of the world or something. As if we really cared.

He blipped to another station. Oh, yeah. A game show. The host had a slicked-back pompadour. His sidekick was a toothy blond whose thick mane swished back and forth whenever she knew the camera was pointing her way.

Futility. Wasted time.

He punched the remote again.

". . . And now this tragic news from Beijing. Twenty million are believed to be dead following the worst natural disaster in written history. A tsunami, whose wave heights reached upwards of one hundred feet, roared up from the southeast, slamming into the port cities of Macau, Shantow, and the former English enclave of Hong Kong. China's government officials, world relief agencies, and United Nations delegates are scrambling to assess the damage and to begin rescue and relief efforts . . . ."

He dropped the remote and stared intently at the screen.

Whoa! This was bad! Since fourth grade when he'd first read and researched the nation of China, he had been fascinated by any news pertaining to that country.

". . . The following scenes may be too graphic and disturbing for some of our viewers. Parental discretion is advised . . . ."

The camera zoomed in on the destruction of buildings, of forests and fields, of beasts and of human life. Muddy rivers of water and debris pulled back to the sea. The water washed away much of the landscape's former beauty and left a desolate scene of mud, decay, and despair. Trees had snapped off. Roofs were wrapped around branches. The dead body of a farm animal, perhaps an ox, bobbed up and down as the swirling current shoved it out of the camera's view.

The boy's hands shook. What a price these people had to pay! What awful, awesome power the earthquake under the ocean's floor had unleashed! But he could bear it no more. He had to escape the sights and sounds of this news broadcast.

He intended to push the power switch.

He missed.

"I'd like to buy a vowel, Tom," the twangy mid-western voice moaned.

Click.

"Don't you raise your voice in this court, young lady!"

"I was just . . . ."

Click.

" I can't imagine life without you, Madeleine."

"Oh, Ramon, I feel the same as . . . ."

Click.

Stuck. Just stuck. Ever wonder why?

1. What is the "tube"? _____ .

2. Which of the following is a synonym of *gumption*? (Circle your choice.)

   muscles   wisdom   spunk   electricity

3. What is **your** meaning for "parental discretion"?_____
   _____

4. If you could counsel this boy about his lack of drive, what might you tell him?

   _____
   _____

5. What do you think the author wants you to see here?

   _____
   _____

6. If you would critique television, what elements would you say make a program good? (Name three.) _____ _____ _____

7. What elements make a program poor? (Name three.) _____
   _____ _____

Black, White, and Read All Over

Okay, so there are all sorts of places to look in your newspaper. Well, what if we gave you eight scripts. Could you figure out what section of the paper they came from? Match each script (headline-less, of course) with its corresponding section at the bottom of the page.

_____ 1. Help! Need a cage for our 12-foot python. Must be of stainless steel wire with reinforced meshing. Minimum size 4' x 4' x 2'. No size too large. Call 289-5PYT.

_____ 2. Area residents are reporting an outbreak of yet another round of monkey flu. Its most noticeable symptoms include fatigue, fever, and an unusual growth of body hair on the shoulders of its victims. The health department of our county recommends a voluntary quarantine to alleviate the problem.

_____ 3. *Powder Horn*—This Davy Crockett movie remake, starring Macaulay Culkin as the legendary Tennessee woodsman, would make John Wayne, Fess Parker, and Clint Eastwood blush. Placing the set in Oslo, Norway, was only one of its milder errors. Don't waste your money here! Rating: 3 tongues out.

_____ 4. Ah, spring! What a pleasure to dig one's hands into the earth. Now is the time to consider the ph level of your soil as you plan your spring planting. Remember that different plants require different soils. For example . . . .

_____ 5. **MORTUUS**—Herman Mortuus, age 94, passed away on Friday, April 2, with his loving family in attendance. He is preceded in death by . . . .

_____ 6. In Brussels today talks resumed between delegates from the Western Republic of Southern Toria and the Greater Achilles. Last week talks were abruptly postponed when the Torian diplomat stepped on the heel of the G. A. official. "We sure got off on the wrong foot," stated Colonel. M. Aye . . . .

_____ 7. Carpentry—licensed 17 years. caring craftsmanship. eager to do your cabinet work. excellent references and referrals. Call 397-60AK.

_____ 8. Wimbledon—Tigress Euphrates, the young tennis sensation quickly becoming the sports heartthrob of the western world, has done it again! This week in three easy sets she smashed Britain's Curdsy Whey, trounced Ghana's Mies Moffet, and fleeced Indiana's Boe Peepe . . . .

Newspaper Sections

a. obituaries	b. entertainment	c. gardening	d. local news
e. services	f. sports	g. want ads	h. world news

Somewhere Out There

Captain Xtfiv Myks of the Unilateral States of Aerio has recently completed his intergalactic mission and in record time! Oddly enough, many of the creatures he discovered are identical to those found on Planet Earth. Directions: Fill in the Venn diagram on the following page correctly to show which creatures are found on which planets.

Planet Pax	**Planet Wax**	**Planet Fax**
ant	ant	ant
beetle	bear	auk
buffalo	buffalo	bear
cat	butterfly	bee
chickadee	cobra	beetle
chipmunk	coral snake	buffalo
cobra	crow	cat
finch	dragonfly	coyote
fly	finch	crow
frog	fly	dragonfly
gnat	frog	fly
jay	leech	frog
minnow	magpie	gecko
mouse	minnow	gopher
pike	mudpuppy	leech
sloth	rabbit	moth
slug	salamander	mouse
swallow	shrimp	salamander
tern	sloth	shrimp
tortoise	snail	swallow
wasp	tern	tern
	tortoise	tortoise
	walrus	wasp

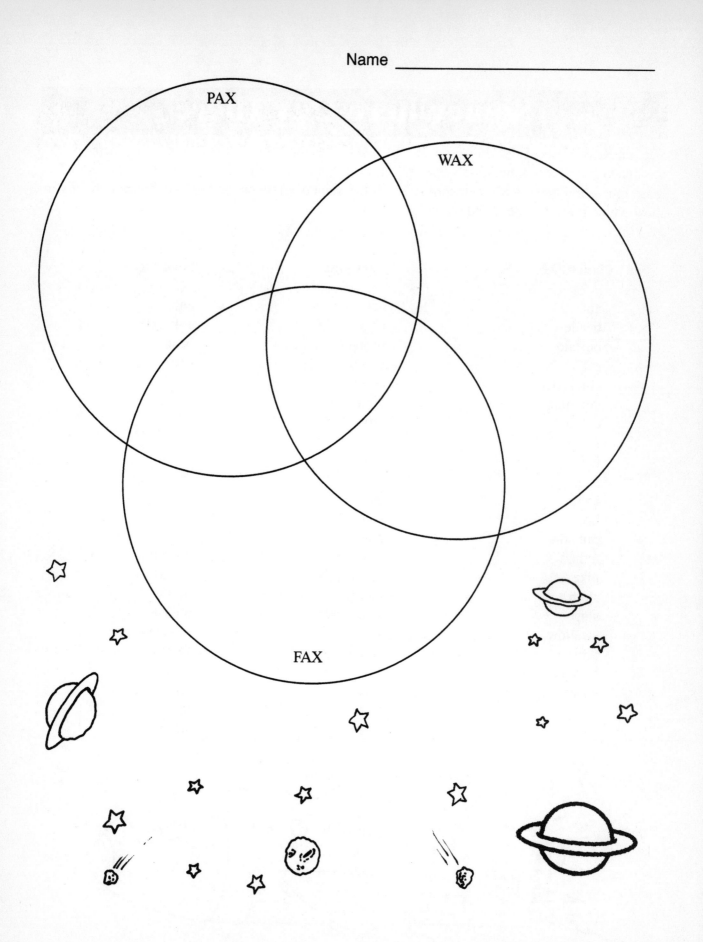

86

It's True!

Some say that Paul Bunyan was the greatest of the shanty boys of the North Woods. Pure hogwash, if you excuse my French. Sure, the kid was tough! Sure, he could swing a mean axe! But greatest? No sir!

My great-uncle, Ole Bergstrom, was the greatest. No one could best him! Ole came to this great nation in the 1860s. He came for the farmland promised in those Old World posters. Ole took my great-aunt, Tante Trina, and they found passage on a small merchant ship out of Oslo. Well, they ran into a terrible storm at sea. The ship's crew couldn't get the engines working hot enough to make any headway. So what to do? Grown men were crying. The captain, bitin' down on his pipe like as to chomp off the stem, called for passenger volunteers . . . "or all souls will be lost," he said. Well, that got me Uncle Ole hopping. He stormed down to the ship's boiler and loaded it with coal faster than the whole crew combined. Knocked three men flat out silly in his hurry. But the ship was freed from the storm's grip and came to this land.

New York City couldna hold Uncle Ole. No, he took Tante Trina and left for the North Woods as soon as his immigration forms were signed. Westward they traveled by rail, by stagecoach, by steamer, and by foot until they reached the Michigan North Woods. I heard tell that when the train derailed in Albany, Uncle Ole lifted it back on the tracks. Now, maybe that was so, but I doubt it. He had a touch of fever after carrying a lame horse 20 miles just east of that city. Twice, mean-spirited thugs tried to rob my uncle and aunt. Twice, bruised and broken-boned roughnecks landed in the local hoosegow.

When Uncle Ole reached his claim, it was April. He wasted no time building a house. No sir. He pulled up four beech trees, braided their trunks into four walls and a snug roof, and set his missus there in a cozy little home with enough firewood to last eight years. I heard it said that one stomp of his foot would clear an acre of trees. Now, don'tcha believe everything you hear! What really happened is that Ole would stomp *both* feet and yell out,"Fall, you puny toothpicks." And it was his breath as much as the earth tremors which knocked the forest flat. So after he cleared the land, he planted wheat, 'tatoes, corn, barley, beans, and that marvelous popcorn. And, oh the farm prospered!

But when the call came for shanty boys to muster, Uncle Ole left the farm, his wife, and his three young babes—for, oh, they prospered!—and hired himself to Mr. Amos Macomb for the winter seasons. Macomb's logging company hired nigh to a hundred hands. Drivers, and sawyers, and road monkeys, and cook, and haulers, foremen, and stable boys. And Ole. Ole could do it all. We later heard all sorts of stories of Great Uncle Ole Bergstrom.

Like when Oscar Dobbers' horse went lame, Ole pulled the load to give the beast a week's rest. From then on the horse would only sleep outside Ole's window.

When a felling crew got lost in a blizzard, Ole not only found them, he built them a snow house and for four days warmed them with his stories until the storm blew out.

When the camp's steam engine sparked a fire which torched the barn, the mess hall, three shanties, and a privy, Ole picked up an empty wagon, repeatedly scooped it full of snow, and dumped it on the fire, forming a huge rock of ice. This newly formed ice mountain Uncle Ole then shaped to form the first ice saw mill in the Americas.

And when the Au Sable River suffered its worst logjam in '82, it was Ole who divined the solution. He ordered all the company's men to melt snow by rolling back and forth in it to raise the river level. Ole himself grabbed a peavey and pounced on the logjam. With wild glee he single-handedly scattered those huge logs, flailing about with his pole as the river rose. Toby O'Nancy claimed the thuds and roars, the cracks and screeches of the jam sounded as if heaven's giants were a'playin' nine-pin. Ole cursed and chortled, laughed and grimaced until all logs were again on their way downstream and the drivers could again guide the load to market.

But this last challenge was the last we heard tell of Uncle Ole. Drivers say he rode the lead logs downstream like George Washington a'crossin' the Delaware. They say he hollered something about River Styx, whatever that is. They say he disappeared around the river bend and was never seen again.

And Tante Trina, she kept mum.

1. Who is the main character?

   _____

2. Where does the tale take place?

   _____

3. When does this happen?

   _____

4. Give three examples of exaggeration.

   _____

   _____

   _____

5. Match the phrases from the story with their definitions on the right by placing the correct letter in each blank.

   _____ a. mum   g. trader
   _____ b. merchant   h. jail
   _____ c. hoosegow   i. lumberjack
   _____ d. privy   j. loggers pole
   _____ e. peavey   k. rustic bathroom
   _____ f. shanty boy   l. quiet

Moving Right Along

Begin your move at **start.** Read each of the 16 directions carefully. If you are correct you will never leave the grid. Show the path you take to reach the prize.

1. If Lisbon is in Spain, move east 4 units. If not, move south 3 units.
2. If a cur is a dog, move west 5 units. If not, move north 3 units.
3. If magenta is a shade of red, move south 1. If not, move north 4.
4. If cirrus is a cloud type, move east 2. If not, move east 6.
5. If Lois Lowry wrote *Howliday Inn,* move south 1. If not, move north 8.
6. If Amelia Earhart was a pilot, move south 2. If not, move west 2.
7. If Charles Barkley plays football, move east 4. If not, move east 7.
8. If a koala is a type of panda, move south 8. If not, move north 3.
9. If a kiwi is a fruit, move east 1. If not, move west 4.
10. If a radish grows underground, move south 5. If not, move west 2.
11. If Bulgaria is in Europe, move west 6. If not, move south 4.
12. If Chad is in Asia, move north 5. If not, move south 5.
13. If whales gather into flocks, move east 6. If not move east 4.
14. If Moses was Harriet Tubman's alias, move north 8. If not, move west 5.
15. If the prophet Mohammed was born in Turkey, move north 2. If not, move west 3.
16. If coffee comes from shrubs, move south 1. If not move east 6.

Start

Oops! Sorry!

Gerry has planned a Friday night party for boys and girls. Each boy was to bring a snack. As Gerry knew, each boy had a crush on one of the girls invited and so brought a snack she would like. The girls reciprocated the affection. Unfortunately, the five invited boys accidentally spilled their snacks on their sweethearts. Can you match the boys, girls, and spilled snacks? Use the grid below to help you reach your decision.

	Fern	Gigi	Hanna	Iola	Jasmine	chips	pop	cookies	carrots/celery	pretzels
Andrew										
Bao										
Charlie										
Don										
Emilio										
chips										
pop										
cookies										
carrots/celery										
pretzels										

	Boy	Girl	Snack
1.	_____	_____	_____
2.	_____	_____	_____
3.	_____	_____	_____
4.	_____	_____	_____
5.	_____	_____	_____

1. Either Iola or Gigi had cookie crumbs plastered on her clothes.
2. Emilio, who does not adore Fern, did not bring cookies.
3. Pretzels or chips are the desire of Bao's heart throb.
4. Either Fern likes Don or Don's match likes pop, but not both.
5. Andrew and Charlie like Gigi and Hanna but not necessarily in that order. Andrew's dear loves pop.
6. Jasmine adores celery and carrots.
7. Iola, who won't touch chips or cookies, is not dreaming of Emilio.

Fee, Fi!

It ain't a lot of fun to be so big. De odder folks jest kinda poke fun of me an' snicker. Dey's all calls me a giant. Sometime dey jest trow fruit or rocks at me an' de missus. Dat be why we decide ta go off an' live in de wilderness bide our own selves.

We not take much, ya know. Like we took our chickens an' kitchen chairs an'table, me harp an'lute, an'de lot of money we got saved. We sold our haus an' everyting else we couldna take. An' being as we were bot' so strong an'big, we eidder carried de lot our own selves or had Moses truck it.

Moses was our tiny burro. 'Tweren't much larger den a shaggy hound but dearer ta me an'de missus den five children. Not dat I dislike wee folk! Oh, no! We jest weren't blessed wid dem an' don't want ta make bones about dat. Why, fee, fi! I'd a smell sometin' evil if I wuz to covet wot lot anodder being had, you know?

We moved our lot up into de hills, high overlookin' our village in de valley. De only way to reach our cave wuz ta climb a grapevine rope han'over han'. We pullt our lot up over de rocks wid rope an' vine an' left Moses to scrounge for hisself. He not run off. Knows his fambly an' love us dear, ya know.

So when de wolves did scarf him away, it were a cruelty to us bot', I tell ya. De wife, she 'bout grieve herself to de grave, she did. But we overcome dis affliction like all odders. I keep us in food by farmin' a wee patch of wheat an' barley, by keepin' a herd o' goats high above. ('Twere wild goats to some, but not to us. I could e'en milk de nannies in time.) An' I would fish an' hunt in de odd moment of freedom.

De wife, she care for our cave an'de chickens. She make de bread an' fix de warm food. Makin' cloak an' warm cloddes did take up much o' her time but still she lonely for human voice. Me too. But I wuz able to walk it away. To de missus 'twas always a grief jest biting at de heart.

So when dis yellow hair kid come up one day from de village, de missus did feed him from our lot. She showed him aroun' de place. So later he did run off an' steal my chicken. Not all. No! But 'twas a bodder jest de same, an' de wife did feel she let us down. Now I was angry. Not wid de wife. No! But wid de boy who steal from my kindly mate. An' I swore I'd have his skull crush I see him again. But I not go into village. Too many bad folk dere.

But de boy come back. Not unnerstan' why for de sake of mercy! But he do. An' he take de money we have save. Neider wife nor me did see him come. But, oh, we see him go! De wife come chase him off an' a'wavin' her broom an' shoutin', "Fie on you. We smell ya! Be off wid your bony self, but have you no more our bread!" Den she cried an' when I come down from de high plain where'd I seed it all, I could jest put de arm around' her an' let her weep. 'Twuz no right, de boy stealin' an' all. An' I wuz set to follow, I wuz so angry.

But de wife say no. De people not care for us. Dey would lie to save dere own. An' de missus, she be right, so I stay. An' we done heal from de pain a bit too.

But a few mont' later de boy come back again. I wuz out huntin' an' he come sneakin' into de cave while de wife's back turn. An' he crouch under table. When I comed in, I smelled dat funny smell of de village an' did remark, "Fie! I smell de English scum." Den I dressed de meat I done brung an' hung it over de fire to dry. De wife wuz a cleanin' me harp an' it were on de table still. So I pluck a few string til 'twuz eatin' time. An' we did sup.

Sudly I sawed dese hands come over de table an' snatch me harp! Away did run de scamp an' I follow him fast an' hard. Oh, I 'bout grab him before he done reach de vine when down he go! Well, I chase after de boy but when he get to village, he yell 'bout me tryin' ta kill him. So I wuz met wid townfolk wavin' dere axes an' pitchforks an' clubs at me.

I yell, "De boy done steal from me an' de missus. He took me chicken, me money, an' me harp. Fie on him! An' fie on you for takin' his side."

But de folk jest laugh an' taunt me like de missus say de would. An' not'ing for to do but go back to de cave an' de missus.

We done leave dat hateful land. We pull up our vine, we grab our lot, an' I take dat boy's cow in de bargain.

Not an' even trade but will do.

1. Number these events in chronological order.

   _____ boy steals harp   _____ burro dies

   _____ giant takes cow   _____ family leaves village

   _____ boy steals money   _____ village people protect boy

   _____ boy steals chicken

2. Label and describe the emotions behind these phrases.
   a. ". . . de odder folks jest kinda poke fun of me an' snicker."

   _____

   b. "But we overcome dis affliction like all odders."

   _____

   c. ". . . I could jest put de arm around her . . ."

   _____

   d. "An' fie on you for takin' his side."

   _____

3. Told from the giant's perspective, the story is quite different from the typical "Jack and the Beanstalk" tale we commonly recite. To you, what are the two most striking differences?
   a. _____

   _____

   b. _____

   _____

Data Doubled

Use the first chart to answer these questions.

1. How many girls are in sixth grade? _____

2. How many boys are in Rooms B and C? _____

3. How many students are in Rooms A and D? _____

4. Are there more girls or boys in sixth grade? _____

5. How many students are there in total? _____

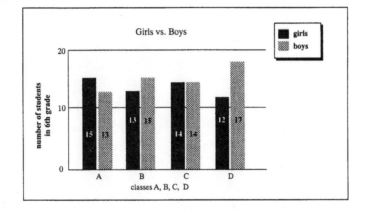

Use the second chart to answer the following questions.

6. Which room has the most students favoring math? _____

7. Which has the most students favoring communications? _____

8. Which room seems most evenly divided? _____

9. Do more students favor math or communications? _____

10. By how many students? _____

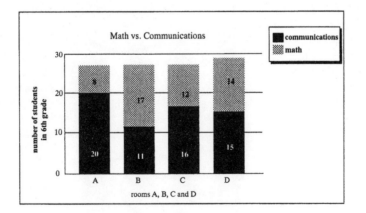

In Your Face

Popsy Peretti begged her parents for permission to explore the new In Your Face Zoo in Bistro, Sri Lanka. The zoo is divided into three pods, namely Reptile Row, Matrix of Mammals, and Bird Boutique.

Although she desired a larger selection of critters and found the pod names ridiculous, Popsy (Hey, who is she to talk?) loved the opportunity to get this close to the animals. In all cases but one, she touched the creatures. So much for wild.

In the Matrix of Mammals, Popsy stroked two members of the cat family, the Siberian tiger and the jaguar. The lynx, in a foul mood, kept its distance. Of the bears the Kodiak, who had just taken an icy dip, had cold, smelly, and wet fur. However, the panda and polar bear, Popsy discovered, had very soft fur.

Reptiles are Popsy's joy. A python curled around her neck, and she fed the glass snake and coral snake with the attendant's assistance. Of the lizards, she found the gila monster most personable. Neither the monitor nor gecko gave her much notice, barely acknowledging her presence. So she left the Row in a huff.

At the Bird Boutique Popsy swam with the wood duck, hid with the ruffed grouse, and chortled with the wild turkey. No wonder they're called "game" birds! The golden eagle and osprey were eating during her visit (pretty graphic!), which was cool. The barred owl, also a predator, sat on Popsy's shoulder and nipped pleasantly at her ear. What a day!

Directions: Fill the web with names of these zoo creatures.

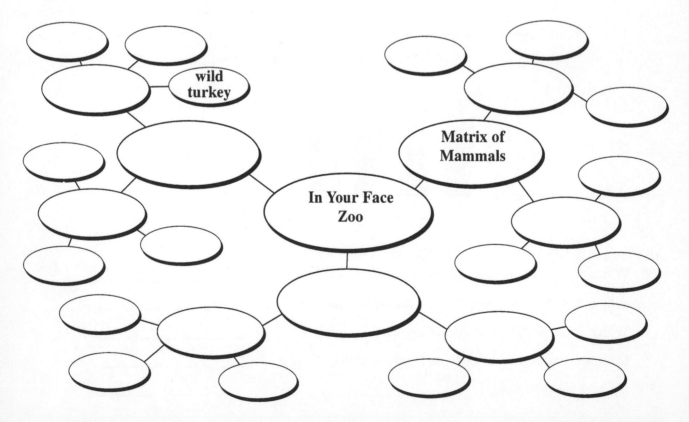

With You

Yeah. Papa was going away tonight. He got to go bowling and roll that heavy ball. Davy could only imagine what a bowling alley looked like. He'd never bowled. But Papa told him about it. Davy had a great idea.

"Hey, Papa, I could go with you! I can bowl . . . and and you could teach me!" Davy pleaded in a singsong voice.

Mama frowned. Papa worked too hard. She knew Papa had tired eyes. And a haggard body. And a weary soul. The last thing he needed was the whining of six-year-old Davy. It was harvest time on the farm. The apples wouldn't stay on the trees much longer. The winds of autumn were already dropping the fruit from the trees. And the nimble-handed workers could not keep up with the red, ripened crop.

But Papa smiled down at Davy.

"So, you'd like to go bowling with me, huh?"

"Oh, Papa, could I?"

Davy could not believe it. Papa had spoken to him! Papa, who was sooo busy, had smiled at him and . . . and . . . and even talked like maybe, just maybe he'd take Davy bowling.

"There's just one thing, Davy," spoke his father. "If I take you, I'll have to take your older brother and sister, too. We couldn't leave them behind, could we?"

Davy had to think about that. He hadn't considered Ben and Tara. Boy, it was a good thing Papa had! Oooh, if Papa had taken him but left them home, they would have been sooo mad! They would have teased him. And punched him. And made him miserable for a jillion years or so.

"Sure, Papa, we could take them too," Davy sang.

So Papa warmed up the old Chevy pickup, and Tara, Ben, and Davy piled in. Davy scooted next to Papa in the cab, and his siblings scrunched in beside him. And away they rode. Five miles into town. To the bowling alley. To Papa's place!

Once, Papa had bowled a perfect game. Three hundred points. Davy didn't know what that meant. But it was good. And Davy was proud of Papa. He hoped Papa could be proud of him, too.

They arrived and entered the old brick building. Smoke was everywhere. Davy's eyes watered. He coughed and sneezed. But, oh, it was great! This was Papa's paradise! This is where grown men met, and laughed, and drank big clear glasses of pop with ice cubes. Davy put on his bowling shoes. Then Papa helped him find a big ol' black ball. It had three holes in it! It was marked with nicks and dents. Davy wondered if it had been a cannon ball during a war. It was soo heavy. Eight pounds, Papa said.

Papa showed the kids how to stand. How to step forward. How to swing back the arm and roll the ball forward. And when Papa's ball went down the alley, it knocked over all ten pins! They just crashed and clinked and spun around, and the ball disappeared. And Tara and Ben shouted, "A strike, Papa! You got a strike!" So Davy hopped up and down, too.

And then Tara and Ben and Davy took turns rolling their balls. And sometimes they would knock over some pins. And sometimes they would get gutter balls. What a funny name. Gutter balls! It almost sounded like swearing to say that word. Gutter balls!

After the first game Papa was beaming. He gave bubble gum to each of his kids. Tara and Ben unwrapped their gum and stuffed it into their mouths. Davy squinched his eyes. He was scared. Bubble gum! Ben had told him how this gum made big, round bubbles. What if the bubble blew up? Would it hurt? Was it scary?

"Papa," said Davy shyly, "no, thanks. I don't need any bubble gum."

"Oh, sure you do, Davy," laughed his dad. "Just put it in your mouth and chew. Look at Ben and Tara. They're chewing."

"But I don't want any bubbles," squeaked Davy.

"Don't worry. If you don't want bubbles, don't blow them. Now go ahead!"

So Davy stuffed his square into his mouth. But the fear of what he couldn't know, the horror of huge, pink bubbles was too much for him. It was all Davy could do to keep from crying right there. In Papa's paradise! In the place with all these big men. And he didn't want to cry. He didn't want to upset Papa.

So chewing carefully, fearfully, almost tearfully, Davy whispered, "Papa, I don't want to bowl anymore. Can we go home?"

Papa peered at his small son incredulously. "But you begged to bowl. I thought we were having fun here."

"Yes, Papa. But now I wanna go home," whispered Davy.

Tara groaned. Ben gave Davy a dirty look. Papa looked downright bewildered.

"Davy, if you don't want to bowl this second game, alright. But the rest of us are going to play. So just sit tight. Don't complain. We want to have some fun here." Davy thought that Papa looked like he might yell. He looked disappointed.

So Davy sat in the smoke. His papa, his sister, and his brother knocked down pins. And they laughed and yelled. And Tara got a spare. And Ben rolled his ball super fast. And Papa spared on a split. And Davy worried about his bubble gum, afraid that it might blow up in his face. But it didn't.

And later they went home. Papa was tired when he tucked Davy into bed.

"Davy," he said, "why did you quit? Didn't you want to bowl?"

Davy couldn't tell his papa about the bubble gum. Papa gave it to him as a present. So he croaked, "Papa, it was just enough to be with you."

Answer these questions.
1. What does Papa do for a living? _____

2. What is Papa's place? _____

3. Davy has a desire or two. What do you think is his greatest desire in this story? Why do you think so?_____

4. What is Davy's fear? _____

5. Why didn't Davy tell his Dad what was bothering him? _____

_____

6. Do you think this is a happy story? A sad story? Why do you think so?_____

_____

A Contractual Agreement

Read the following contract.

The owners of *Sports Freaks* at 1968 Lolich Lane do hereby agree to hire *The Green Thumb Lawncare Services* and pay them for services rendered under the conditions that follow.

The Green Thumb Lawncare Services agrees to:

A
1. mow weekly beginning the third full week of April and continue for 24 weeks through the first week of October.
2. edge all business driveways and sidewalks monthly.
3. trim grass from around trees, bushes, signs, and statues.
4. remove or blow all loose grass clippings from driveways and walkways.
5. provide aforementioned lawn care either on Monday or Tuesday of each week between the hours of 8:30 a.m. and 5:30 p.m.

In return *Sports Freaks* agrees to:

B
1. make payments in timely, monthly order by the fifteenth of each month beginning May 15 for a total of six payments of $200 each.
2. keep gates open and the grounds accessible for the ground crew's work. Any additional work (bush trimming or fall leaf collection, for example) will be handled under a separate contract.

Signatures: *Mitch Melville* _____   *March 13, 20__ __* _____
               president of *Sports Freaks*   date
               Perry Winkle _____   *March 13, 20__ __* _____
               treasurer, *The Green Thumb Lawncare Services*   date

Questions:

1. Approximately how long before service began was this contract signed?

   2 weeks   4 weeks   6 weeks   8 weeks

2. What is the address of the business to be cared for? _____

3. How many payments will be made? _____

4. Who is Mitch Melville? _____

5. Must the lawn service trim bushes? _____

6. Why must Sports Freaks agree to B2? _____

7. What is the total payment by Sports Freaks for services rendered? _____

8. Who signed this contract on Green Thumb's behalf? _____

9. How many weeks will the service work? _____

10. On what days of the week must the lawn care do their work? _____

Extra: If you were the owner of Sports Freaks, what additional requirement might you suggest?

_____

Students in Sports

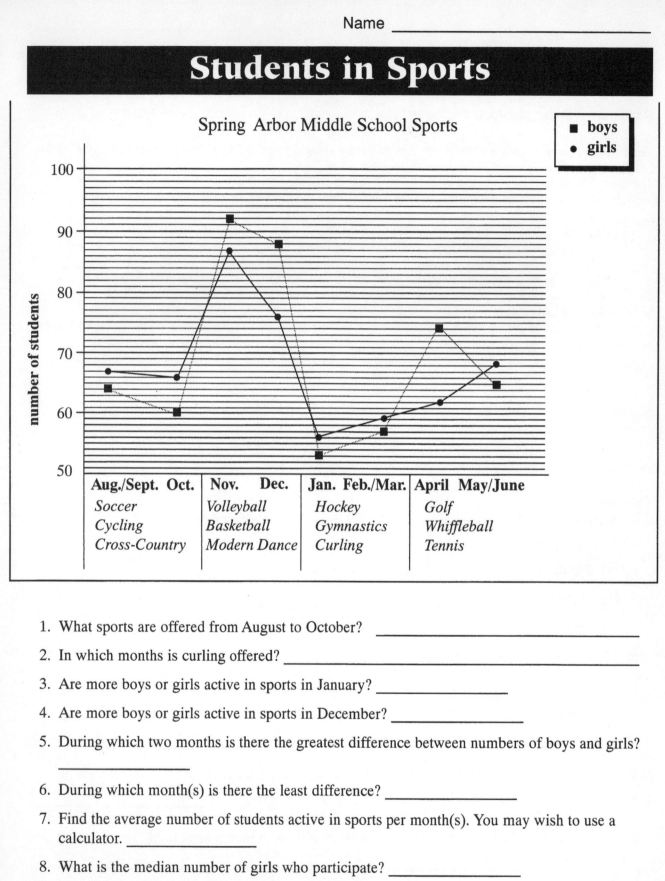

Spring Arbor Middle School Sports

■ boys
● girls

number of students

100

90

80

70

60

50

Aug./Sept. Oct.	Nov. Dec.	Jan. Feb./Mar.	April May/June
Soccer	*Volleyball*	*Hockey*	*Golf*
Cycling	*Basketball*	*Gymnastics*	*Whiffleball*
Cross-Country	*Modern Dance*	*Curling*	*Tennis*

1. What sports are offered from August to October? _____

2. In which months is curling offered? _____

3. Are more boys or girls active in sports in January? _____

4. Are more boys or girls active in sports in December? _____

5. During which two months is there the greatest difference between numbers of boys and girls? _____

6. During which month(s) is there the least difference? _____

7. Find the average number of students active in sports per month(s). You may wish to use a calculator. _____

8. What is the median number of girls who participate? _____

9. What is the median number of boys who participate? _____

How'd You Like That?

Here's food for thought. Today in most world communities, if you're hungry for meat, you go to a restaurant or food market, pick up your beef, pork, mutton, fowl, or fish, and simply return home. Even families who enjoy hunting buy most of their meat. Of course, that wasn't always so.

In times and places where agriculture was unknown or unavailable, humans had to hunt to survive. One such people were the Native Americans of the Great American Plains. These well-practiced hunters consumed antelope, rabbit, fish, and quail, but their primary food source was bison. The trick, of course, was bringing down the beast.

With gunpowder and rifle still unknown in the Americas, these hunters used their spear and javelin. They utilized the bow, too. But hunting bison is no easy walk through the park. Remember, bison are large creatures. They can travel with arrows protruding from their sides just as you can run off after you've been stung by a bee. Well, not exactly, but you get the idea. An arrow must hit its target squarely to do its work. As well, bison could travel with speed, and the hunters, horseless before Coronado's travels, were hard pressed to keep up. The stubborn and ornery adult bison was no easy prey for the unskilled hunter.

Imagine a young hunter who has trekked 20 or more miles unaccompanied across the grassy plains in search of his first bison kill. He walks and walks until finally, climbing over a grassy knoll, he sees before him a herd of a hundred thousand bison. His sudden appearance startles them. A few adult bison turn to stare briefly before instigating the thunderous stampede which in minutes leaves the hunter alone once more. Can you imagine the gibes of his people when he returns to his village? Or their bitter disappointment in hunger?

We know that hunters of these plains sometimes wore skins of animals to cover their scent and hide their human features. The hide of coyote and wolf could be draped over one's body. Though these canine were no friend of the bison, their presence would be of little alarm to the adult herd, who knew well how to protect their young. So, with weapons in hand, fur-covered hunters could creep within range of the bison and calmly, expertly, drop the beasts in quick, silent, arrow-induced death while the multitude of creatures nonchalantly grazed on.

A most remarkable method of hunting bison is yet to be explained. Hunters searching for bison near rivers sometimes came upon cliffs and bluffs into which river water had cut deep grooves. If these hunters were fortunate to find bison herds nearby, they formed a human corral of people with hunters forming the two side "fences." A noisy, boisterous lot of hunters would startle the beasts and drive them forward, and the bison, attempting to avoid the human wall of hunters, would pass between the two fences. Those hunters on the wall had a most dangerous duty. They had to hold their ground despite the anguishing bellow of bison desperately seeking to escape. If all went as planned, bison would rush toward the cliff's edge and, unable to stop, would tumble to their death. Others would be trampled to death by their desperate kin. Some would finally escape through the fences of hunters who had already obtained all the meat they could use.

After a kill like this, hunters and their families would feast on fresh meat. They would skin the dead creatures and save what body parts they might use for clothing, shelter, tools, and food. And how recent an invention is this technique? A site has been found in Colorado suggesting that Native Americans practiced it 8,500 years ago!

Now that's food for thought.

Questions:

1. Who is this article about? _____

2. What was their chief source of food? _____

3. What was the difficulty of killing the animal? _____

   _____

4. How might the hunters camouflage themselves? _____

   _____

5. What formed the "fence" described here? _____

6. How did hunting change with the arrival of the Europeans? _____

   _____

7. Find in the article a synonym for the words *noisy* or *raucous*. _____

8. Find in the article a synonym for the word *crevices*. _____

9. Find the homophone for the word *sent*. _____

What's the Word?

Directions: Follow the directions below to discover the mystery word below. You certainly may use a dictionary. Then, write a synonym or short definition for the boldly printed word.

1. If you are **vacuous,** write F. If not, write J.   _____
2. If **tedium** is boring, write U. If not, write A.   _____
3. If a **spud** grows underground, write B. If not, write T.   _____
4. If you can ride a **umiak,** write I. If not, write U.   _____
5. If **infamy** is wonderful, write H. If not, write L.   _____
6. If a **fez** is an animal, write S. If not, write A.   _____
7. If a soldier should be **unwary,** write O. If not, write T.   _____
8. If **brawn** refers to fish, write C. If not, write I.   _____
9. If a **vial** holds liquid, write O. If not, write M.   _____
10. If a **respite** is a ghost, write V. If not, write N.   _____

___ ___ ___ ___ ___ ___ ___ ___ ___ ___
 1   2   3   4   5   6   7   8   9   10

Is that a fez?

Pop Out

Yeah, while he drove the blue Ford tractor lickety-split down the gravel road or through the field, Papa let Kate, me, Ted, and Maddie ride the single-axle trailer.

It was fun! We'd stand up daredevil, trying to keep our balance while Papa drove like crazy, zigzagging this way and that. When somebody'd fall off into the grass, the rest of us hooted and hollered and urged the fallen to catch up before we'd leave 'em behind. While he always slowed down *a little,* Papa had this twinkling eye and sneaky little grin like maybe he'd like to've left the kid in the dust.

Oh, it was fun!

We had one wooden trailer that was goofy. It had a built-in long tool box that stretched out over the wagon and above the axle. The box had two doors for putting tools away. The little ones loved riding in that cubby. Must've been dark. Dirty. Tight. Bumpier than all get out. Just the place for some crazy little kid, huh?

When Papa toted us over the farm to work, we had this game we'd play. We'd stand on the tail edge of the trailer with our heels hanging out behind and we'd balance the best we could. It was easy to fall off. The trailer was extra bouncy back there. And Papa seemed to hit every bump. And *maybe* we wanted to fall off sometimes. You know how people sometimes try to fall? Well.

So, one day Papa got us all together to work with him. We were to haul wood to the house for the fireplace. Cut wood. From trees off beyond the corn and pasture. That meant we could ride on the trailer. Kate and I, we played daredevil standing on the wee back. Ted and Maddie chose to hide themselves away in that silly wooden tool box.

The wood lot was way out across the farm. My, oh my! But we had the ride of our lives. Papa drove over *every* bump on the way but Kate and me, we never fell off. Not once! The two little squeakers howled and groaned every time Papa bounced us over a rock. Sounded like they were dying of toothaches the way they bellowed. Papa charged over hill and dale, reeling around gullies, and so on but we wouldn't fall off. Papa was impressed. I could tell.

There was one last steep incline, and Papa revved up the tractor, nudging the throttle a tad. Kate and me, balancing on the back, must have outweighed the front of the trailer 'cuz suddenly the linchpin—the pin holding the trailer to the tractor—well, it popped out.

Then all sorts of things happened.

Papa raced along on the Ford.

The trailer, when its forward force vanished, ceased its forward motion, and began speeding backward in a drunken, uncontrolled manner.

Kate and I jumped off to one side as the trailer rushed past us.

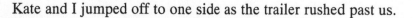

The small door to the tool box snapped open, and a head popped out. Teddy. With eyes opened wide in surprise he shot out of that box like a pea out of a shooter. Maddie followed in perfect imitation.

Both fell free of the miscreant wagon.

Papa zipped along.

We all hollered for Papa to halt.

The trailer charged to the bottom of the hill and came to rest against the trunk of an apple tree.

We hollered some more and Papa must've heard us. He stopped and came back to retrieve us.

We still love riding daredevil on the trailer. And Papa still drives the tractor like a bat outa Hades. But I've never seen anybody pop out of a box like Ted and Maddie. Their eyes were bugging out clear to Kalamazoo.

Kate calls it a knee slapper.

1. Match these terms from the story with their meanings:
   a. lickety-split _____
   b. daredevil _____
   c. hoot and holler_____
   d. cubby _____
   e. all get out_____
   f. tote _____
   g. squeakers _____
   h. revved _____
   i. linchpin _____
   j. miscreant _____
   k. bug out_____

Meanings:

villainous	small enclosure	high-pitched little kids	quickly
open wide	sped	anything you could imagine	metal bolt
dangerously	yell loudly	transport	

2. Circle the genre of literature you believe this story is. (Choose only one!)

   fantasy   science fiction   fiction   biography   poetry

   Give the reason for your choice. _____

   _____

3. What might Ted and Maddie have thought as they left the tool box?

   " _____ "

Sanitation Engineer

Fill in the blanks below with words from the Word Bank. You will use each word one time.

"Sean, get your (1)_____ up here and clean up this (2)_____!"

"Aw, Mom! I just got home from a hard day at school. Can't I have some time to (3)_____?"

"Hey, Kiddo, you told me last week you'd clean up this mayhem by (4) _____.
Now it's Tuesday. You've got to get rid of it."

Groaning as (5) _____as a granny's rocker (voice change, you know), Sean

clumped up the stairs. He carried a bowl of Oreos, a liter of Pepsi, and a half bag of cheese curls.

"Mom, you're as (6) _____ as a drill sergeant . . . ."

". . . Hey! Now what are you (7) _____ with more food here? You put that

(8) _____ and scrape up this stuff. NOW!"

(9) _____ his blunder, Sean clumsily set his snacks on the hallway

(10) _____. He took the wet cloth and garbage bag his mom held out to him and

began to (11) _____ the crusted remains of chocolate pudding and moldy apple

slices from his bedroom floor, the four-month-old remains of a peanut butter-and-jelly sandwich

(12) _____ on his desk, the empty chip bags and (13) _____ boxes

scattered about, and the hamburger and fries (14) _____ from Major Meatiest

which glowed spectrally above his lamp shade.

"Uh, huh! And don't leave this room 'til I say so," his mother (15) _____

victoriously as she flicked a cheese curl into her grinning (16) _____.

Word Bank	
cereal	doing
grouchy	loudly
mouth	myself
table	tackle
down	gloated
lying	mess
Realizing	Saturday
tail	wrappers

IF8719 Reading Comprehension

Drive Like Jehu

When I was little, I went to this Bible school class every summer. It was a two-week program. We'd come into the church and sing songs. We'd hear a Bible story, make some craft dealie, and play outdoor games. I liked it all . . . although I was too self-conscious to admit to liking those crafts. The Bible stories were alright, too. Especially those gruesome and bloody action stories about the old kings. And a soldier general named Jehu.

And that's where my dad comes in.

Okay. I'll back it up again. Jehu was this guy who drove his chariot like he was in the Indy 500. No one could keep up with him. And he was crazy enough that no one would even try. You see, he had a good eye for shooting his bow. But, oh man, his driving was something else to see!

Okay. My dad drives fast, too. He makes it a point to be on time for everything. Doesn't matter when he starts. He always reaches his destination punctually. A coupla times he got my heart fluttering up in my throat, and there is the story of my mom falling out of a moving pickup truck. But, oh, could he fly!

Which is the point of my story.

To get to our high school, my sister and I would first hitch a mile ride to our bus stop. That's all the closer the school bus could come. Usually my sister and I would squash ourselves into the cab of Dad's Chevy pickup, and he'd book it to the corner. Did this most every day. Rain or shine. Snow or ice. Winter, spring, or fall. Got the picture?

Okay. We had this terrible ice storm this winter. Maybe you heard of it? Caused roads to crumble all over the district. Knocked the power out for days. Schools too . . . . But we gotta make up those days, school says. So already the driving's been dicey around here. Then two nights ago we had a torrential rain. Didn't even think about it.

Neither did Dad.

Okay. We had a late start for our clip to the corner next morning. Laina had to get some last-minute stuff from the kitchen for her all-important science project. But we dashed to the warmed-up Chevy where Dad was waiting and crowded inside it. Okay. Dad near to floored the pedal once he got to the main road. I swear he tries to break his speed record every time he gets behind the wheel! We two kids just kinda hung our heads to doze for our ritual one- or two-minute snooze.

Now unbeknownst to us, the night rain had destroyed the road ahead. Where the road stretches over a culvert, rushing water had washed away ¾ of the road, creating a crevice ten feet across and 4 to 8 feet deep.

Barreling toward this hole was my daring dad. Faster and faster he forced the Chevy. Wet tires sang, spewing water aside. "Drives like Jehu," I muttered under my breath.

Okay. It was dark and misty. Dad couldn't see the gully's gap until we were maybe two stone throws away. Quick as a wink he figured he had two choices. Either he could slam on the brakes and probably skid into the chasm, or he could speed up and most likely fall into the abyss. And in another wink he made up his mind. Dad's foot jammed that pedal all the way through the floor, our heads whipped back in response, and we rocketed closer and closer to the void. Dad's tongue peeked out as he concentrated on his mission. My eyes 'bout near to popped out. Laina . . . shoot! Laina actually fell asleep!

I had this picture in my head of Tennyson's Light Brigade riding into the Valley of Death. But oh! We didn't have half a league! The pickup truck screamed. Wind whistled into the less-than-tightly-sealed windows. When we got to the brink of the cavity, I closed my eyes. And on we soared.

I remember the sensation one gets when taking a running leap off a sand dune. That moment of suspension. Floating. And then a slight bump, just a bump, and we were over Death Valley.

Without a spoken word, Dad slowed down and we eased to the bus stop. The bus arrived two minutes later. I woke Laina, got out of the truck, and took the bus to school. The rest of yesterday is hazy. Couldn't talk about the ride to anybody. Maybe it was just too much like a dream.

But last evening Dad and I took another look at the crevice.

"We jumped that?" I tremored.

"Sure couldn't do it again," Dad managed. He shook his head.

"Yeah, you could," I bragged. "You drive like Jehu."

1. Where do you think this story took place?

   city   forest   desert   expressway   rural area   suburb   parking lot

   Why do you think so? _____

   _____

2. What does punctually mean?   rapidly   timely   surely   frequently

3. Who is Jehu? _____

   _____

4. Name three synonyms the author uses for the word *chasm*.

   _____   _____   _____

5. What is a culvert?   waterfall   valley   slope   drainpipe

6. How does the writer's attitude change from early in the story to the end?

   _____

7. How is the boy's father like Jehu? _____

   _____

Top Secret

This coded letter has just been treated with onion juice by our cryptographers to enable our Washington team to read it. Really! It contains boldly printed words written with letters in disarray. Decode those words to help the government in this top-secret project. Remember, mum's the word.

Terry

ˌyours Sincerely

.week-mid by ".Inc ˌMovers" from suit law a expect We .them warned I "ˌpackage the lift you when backs your **reujin** (1) _____ don't Please" .movers local hired We .carry to **bercumsome** (2) _____ too package the found We .Vegas Las to container this send and vault lined-**teeroncc** (3) _____ a in contaminants the seal must we decided I .ruling a make to compelled was ˌleader team as ˌI **clodaked** (4) _____ bitter a in team the With .discovery our about noisily **gleanwr** (5) _____ to began team alpha The .were they what learn to attempt an in book **feerrceen** (6) _____ a used We .**wlwhiirnsd** (7) _____ miniature like about spun creatures celled-one The !**gheenyi** (8) _____ proper practiced has never Erskin Dr. ˌcourse Of .skin Erskin's Dr. invaded **atrabcei** (9) _____ microscopic strange ˌprobe our began we As .events **tracnloun** (10) _____ were tests our reasons obvious For .weeks recent in center control disease our to come have complaints of number **xcesvisee** (11) _____ An .code in you to information this pass must I ˌ**cruseyit** (12) _____ national of sake the For

:President Mrs. Dear

Hit or Myth

The names of mythological Greek characters are encrypted below. Break the code (or use information books) to discover who they are!

1. _____	RGB	god of nature
2. _____	RLCVJALB	god of the sea
3. _____	RXLPVNUVTC	creator of humans
4. _____	TXGBTC	the sky
5. _____	GXNVPJC	goddess of the hunt
6. _____	UVFJLC	god of the sun
7. _____	UGAVC	god of the dead
8. _____	AVPVNVX	goddess of the harvest
9. _____	WSWFLRC	one-eyed smiths who make thunderbolts
10. _____	GNFGC	son of a Titan; carries the vault of the sky on his shoulders
11. _____	HVTC	mightiest god; god of thunder
12. _____	GRLFFL	god of light
13. _____	WVBNGTX	half-horse, half-human
14. _____	USAXG	nine-headed monster
15. _____	UVXG	queen of Olympia
16. _____	GNGFGBNG	swift-running huntress
17. _____	UVXPVC	messenger of the gods
18. _____	GRUXLAJNV	goddess of love
19. _____	LXJLB	giant hunter
20. _____	PJBLNGTX	half-bull, half-human
21. _____	UVXGWFVC	strongest man ever, Zeus' son
22. _____	GXVC	god of war
23. _____	KGVG	the Earth
24. _____	GNUVBG	goddess of wisdom

Stormy Weather

Throughout the afternoon Tad felt this peculiar sensation. During research time in the media center, the air was thick and sweaty. When he worked with his study team planning a math presentation, his room was so stiflingly hot, Tad thought he was in a tropical rainforest. The school day fortunately came to a close, and he escaped outdoors to catch whatever breeze was there.

Wasn't a long walk home. Just four blocks. But today's mood was eerie. No birds singing. The world drooped in silence. All solemnly still. The clouds were charcoal gray and darkening quickly. Three large raindrops splattered to the sidewalk.

"Oh, shoot!" thought Tad. "It's going to be a soaker."

Not that he minded getting wet. Just something to complain about. Griping was natural.

Now the street lights switched on. A whispering stir of wind rattled the maple seeds in the trees. And now a sudden gust of wind nearly pulled Tad's Pepsi cap from his carrothead. Tad clapped his paw over it just in time.

A growing, rolling rumble of thunder told Tad a storm was coming soon. The crisp clap of thunder startled him just the same. Pulling his backpack strap tight and shoving his cap firmly on, Tad began his mad dash toward home.

Now the wind howled.

Lightning slashed into a spruce tree two houses ahead and neatly trimmed the uppermost ten feet from the arboreal cone. The needled branch slipped down down down through the boughs and parked itself inches in front of Tad's dashing form.

"Oh, Mommy!" howled Tad as he hurtled the broken bough.

Embarrassed by his less-than-macho outburst, the boy paused his flight. He glanced left, glanced right. Had anyone heard his cry? He wondered . . . Whoa! He saw it before it came. A glistening, silver wall—that was the only way to describe it—a wall of rain water speeding at him. No escape. None. In less time than it takes to flinch, the gale blasted into Tad. Soaked to the skin instantly.

Breathing in particles of precipitation, Tad picked up the pace.

The wind roared on. Branches cracked and tumbled about. A mighty oak tree blew over across a power line which sparked as it stretched and split.

"Oh, Lordy, Lordy," moaned Tad.

He was soaked and fearful and winded and shaken. He ran through the storm. The last two blocks.

Fumbling with the key, he stood in the wind-whipped wet and finicked and fanagled with the lock until he gained entrance.

Dropped off the backpack, its rivelets of rain rolling onto the entrance tiles. Shucked off the jacket. Shuffled out of the soggy Adidas.

Tad trounced into the kitchen and stopped. There on the floor crouched Pepper. The tail-tapping dog was wet and frightened. She whimpered and trembled as if in anticipation of her master's wrath.

"Hey, girl. Why are you wet, huh?"

And then he knew.

"Oh, man!"

He had let Pepper outside that morning to do her thing. Forgot to let her back in. Obviously, so had the rest of the family. She had remained outdoors until the electrical storm frightened her into a frenetic frenzy and forced her to jump through a screened window off the den. She shook and bowed her head submissively as Tad reached out his hand.

"Aw, poor girl. It's alright," crooned Tad, petting her. "We're safe now."

1. Number these events in proper chronological order.

_____ Tad discovers Pepper.

_____ Tad leaves school.

_____ He uses his keys.

_____ He researches in the media center.

_____ A treetop is hit by lightning.

_____ Tad let Pepper outdoors.

_____ Street lights turn on.

2. List four phrases which describe the weather condition. _____

_____

_____

3. In three sentences tell about a time when you had a weather "adventure."

_____

_____

_____

Haste Makes Waste

Fill in the blanks below with words from the Word Bank.

Word Bank				
apparently	appreciate	civilly	complaints	contact
cosmetic	cost	entrance	finely	gouged
haste	in	inside	June	Movers
neighboring	repair	slid	slogan	Steinway

467 Poetry Lane
Cedar Rapids, IA
(1) _____ 9, 2004

Acme Piano (2) _____, Inc.
808 Hefty Drive
Brooklyn, NY

Dear Sirs:

I (3) _____ your prompt attention and service as you moved our (4) _____ piano for our family from New York City to Cedar Rapids this past April. Your (5) _____ "No One's Faster" seems most appropriate.

However, I do have a small list of (6) _____ to make. First, in taking our (7) _____-tuned instrument from our apartment in upper Manhatten, your movers (8) _____ a 6' x 12' hole in the wall rather than remove the piano through the service (9) _____ as I had requested. Cost to me: $2,350.

Second, according to our (10) _____ apartment dwellers and the police, the piano (11) _____ out of your company's moving van not once but twice because your workers failed to strap it (12) _____ place. Cost of structural (13) _____ to piano legs: $3,200. (14) _____ of tuning: $890. Cost to replace sounding board: $6,620. Cost of (15) _____ repair to piano exterior: $1,480.

Finally, in their (16) _____ to leave our apartment, the movers (17) _____ left an entire Acme Piano Movers uniform, socks, work shoes, and gloves (18) _____ the piano! Cost of mental anguish: $1,200.

I hope we are able to settle this matter (19) _____. I request that you compensate me $15,740 for damages. Should you choose to fight my claim, my lawyer will (20) _____ you in seven days.

Sincerely yours,

F. Sharpe, Doctor of Musicology

London's Calling

For each problem circle the word which does not belong with the other three. Then take the chosen letter from the circled word and place it in the blanks below to discover the mystery phrase.

1.	clarinet	viola	harp	piano	(1st letter)
2.	Hansel	Riding Hood	wolf	grandmother	(2nd)
3.	pear	plover	pickle	pumpkin	(2nd)
4.	trial	lawyer	align	proof	(2nd)
5.	bud	root	branch	bone	(2nd)
6.	cooperate	follow	share	harmonize	(1st)
7.	volleyball	football	tennis	Ping-Pong	(4th)
8.	score	gross	dozen	fifth	(5th)
9.	Macbeth	Lowry	Paulsen	Cleary	(5th)
10.	papier mâché	clay	bowl	paint	(3rd)
11.	Libya	Lithuania	Liberia	Lisbon	(2nd)
12.	strait	ocean	island	bay	(3rd)
13.	mackerel	squid	barracuda	salmon	(5th)

The __ __ __ __   __ __   __ __ __   __ __ __ __

      1 2 3 4   5 6   7 8 9   10 11 12 13

Challenge: Who is responsible for the mystery phrase title? _____

The Visit

I was so nervous.

I hadn't been back there since I was born. And though I knew of many of the people we would see —Dad and Mom often talked about them—there was only one family I really remembered. Abbie's. She was my best friend in fourth grade. Her family came to our country so her parents could study at the university here. Abbie and I were so close! We'd giggle, and learn our times tables, and watch videos, and talk about those stupid boys, and shoot hoops. We shared our secret thoughts and our young, naive dreams.

But that was three years ago and people change. I wondered what if Abbie no longer told those silly garlic jokes? What if we had nothing to say? Nothing in common anymore?

Mom had me during Dad's college training. Dad was interested in foreign languages and wanted to learn more about their customs. Mom learned a lot about the country, too. But Mom says that she spent most of her time worrying about me. And I wasn't even born yet, for pity's sake! Mom didn't trust some of that country's foods. "No nutrition and processed like dog food to boot," she'd say. So she often made soups and salads the way we like them. Mom said that the hospital where I was born was alright. The staff was kind and helpful, condescendingly so, during my delivery. When I was born the staff thought I was cute in a foreign sort of way. You know, the way people think that refugee kids from war-torn countries are cute.

So during our visit I was worried about people staring at me. And I had my reasons! In some of the stores, shoppers stopped and stared. So rudely! When Mom and I talked to each other, folks froze and listened, turning their heads to hear us better. Did they think we'd discuss military secrets or what? I had the feeling that everyone was watching me. Kinda like they didn't trust us but mostly like we were exotic animals on display at the zoo.

Well, we made our rounds of visits to those people Mom and Dad knew. Got hugs and kisses from "uncles" and "aunts" I only remembered through letters. You know, it's not so bad with the hugs and stuff. I just imagine I'm hugging someone's pet. I probably won't ever see them again anyway. Dad lectured at two or three colleges. He got a lot of praise. Meanwhile, I fidgeted.

Oh! I really wanted to see Abbie. I wanted to have back those fun times we once had. Giggle under the bedcovers at night. Laugh at my dad's silly jokes. Pretend that we were sisters. But then, I thought some more. Maybe we'd hate each other now. What if we had nothing to talk about? What if Abbie got really pretty and snobbish? I fidgeted some more.

We drove to Abbie's town, stopping about an hour away to call them. Let them know we were on our way. When we got to their house, the whole family was outside waiting for us. Both her parents, her goofy brother Alex, and . . . Abbie! She was taller (but so was I). Her face was thinner than it used to be. But her smile was the same!

We said hi. And we hugged. Kinda tight. But kinda foreign too, you know?

And then we all trooped inside and sat down. Our parents talked about our families and how we had changed. And about mutual friends. Abbie and I just sat and smiled. Awkwardly. Silently. Then Abbie got a sick feeling in her stomach and had to lie down. And I got a sick stomach but didn't tell anyone. And it was a lousy visit. For me. For Abbie. Things were different. We were different. Strangers. Although we spent the night together and slept in the same room . . . for old time's sake, we probably spoke no more than 50 words to each other. Total. The whole time. I didn't know what to say or how to act.

I'm glad I'm back in Costa Rica. Americans are alright, I guess. And Abbie didn't turn into a snob like I feared she might. But it hurts to be strangers with someone who was my best friend. Maybe this was our final good-bye. It hurts. We are pulled apart by customs and language and experience and appearance. I'm only 12, but I feel so old. Things just aren't the same.

1. From what country does the writer come? _____

2. Where was the writer born? _____

3. Why did her mother prepare her own soups and salads?_____

4. Why did the writer feel like an exotic animal? _____

5. Why was the writer nervous? _____

6. People say they'll be friends forever. List two or three reasons why this may not be possible.

   _____

7. What might you talk to your friends about?_____

8. The writer writes, "I feel so old." Why might she feel this way? _____

9. When have you felt much older than your years? _____

10. If your parents took you to a foreign country, what are some things that could cause you anxiety?_____

Three Cases

1. Daryl Dogoodly, a doting father, had three penniless children. He pulled out 60 dollars and divided it among them. The first received half the money, the second got ³⁄₁₀ of the money, and the third acquired ⅕. A swindling uncle contrived to obtain four dollars from each child, claiming that he required wart surgery. Luckily, soon after this rip-off each child found a sum of money, one in the parking lot, one in a school locker, and the third in a bag of potato chips. The amount each found was equivalent to one-half the money which he or she still held. How much money does each child have now?

	fraction	$	-$4	+½$	new total
first					
second					
third					

2. Lydia Lordly, an ecology-minded landowner, planted five trees: a larch, a white pine, a cedar, a hemlock, and a spruce. She noted that the trees were of five different heights. The spruce was taller than the pine but shorter than the cedar. The larch and the hemlock were neither the two tallest trees nor the shortest. The only conifer to shed its leaves (needles) yearly was of median height. Place the trees in order from tallest to shortest.

3. Bob, Rob, and Robby are of three generations of the Roberts family. In some order they are grandparent, parent, and child. Bob is the parent of at least one of the others. Robby has neither father nor son. Rob has a mother. How are the three related? Hint: Exactly one of the three is a woman.

name   relation

_____   _____

_____   _____

_____   _____

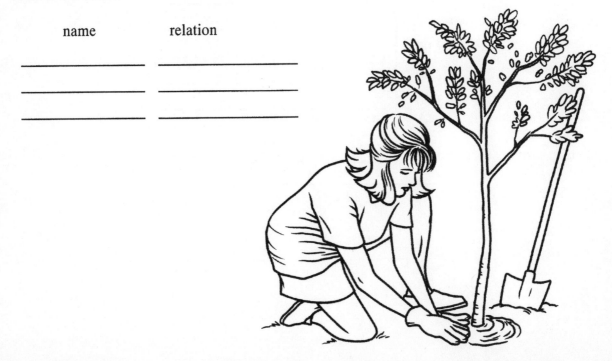

She's in the Money

Every half hour Miss Meredith Moneypenny, through clever investments, watches her holdings grow by $8.00. If the market begins at 8:00 a.m. and closes at 4:00 p.m. and if at 1:00 p.m. her shares are worth $2,718, how much did she own at the market's opening? _____
At the market's closing? _____
By how much did her earning grow during the day? _____

Complete the chart below to answer these questions.

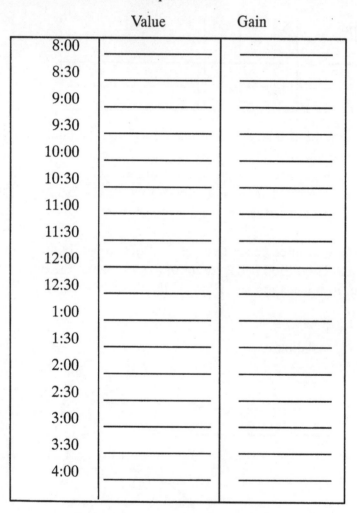

	Value	Gain
8:00	_____	_____
8:30	_____	_____
9:00	_____	_____
9:30	_____	_____
10:00	_____	_____
10:30	_____	_____
11:00	_____	_____
11:30	_____	_____
12:00	_____	_____
12:30	_____	_____
1:00	_____	_____
1:30	_____	_____
2:00	_____	_____
2:30	_____	_____
3:00	_____	_____
3:30	_____	_____
4:00	_____	_____

Answer Key

Little My Wants
page 2
- A. 5, 7, 2, 9, 3, 8
- B. Answers will vary.
- C. Answers will vary.
- D. Answers will vary.

In the Cupboard
page 3
1. author
2. responsible
3. figures
4. special
5. Iroquois
6. natural
7. believe
8. frightened
9. soldier
10. journey
11. contributes
12. everyone

Historical Fantasy

Can You Tell a Book by Its Cover?
page 4
1. j
2. o
3. f
4. b
5. p
6. u
7. a
8. i
9. v
10. e
11. n
12. s
13. x
14. m
15. y
16. r
17. l
18. d
19. h
20. w
21. q
22. c
23. t
24. k
25. g

Moody Blues
page 5
1. c
2. e
3. a
4. b
5. d
6. i
7. h
8. j
9. f
10. g
11. n
12. l
13. o
14. m
15. k

Spinnin' Wheels
page 6
1. Corrie Katik
2. Tootsie Rolls
3. 2 hr 20 min
4. the dog
5. caterpillar diseases
6. All-Flakes Bowl Inn
7. 45 min
8. Anthropology 312
9. 10 min
10. 12:37

Just Friends
page 8
1. he missed his bus
2. Micah—Jake's older sister
   Jeanie—"friend" from school
3. wasn't watching traffic, didn't notice the rain falling
4. Answers will vary.
5. Answers will vary.
6. cruise, hike, sauntered, strode
7. Answers will vary.

RU->
page 9
1. DO
2. CATS
3. REALLY
4. HAVE
5. NINE
6. LIVES?

Niños y Niñas
page 10
Alberto 13
Bonita 12
Ernesto 10

Tune Time Headlines
page 11
1. c
2. i
3. a
4. h
5. d
6. l
7. b
8. k
9. f
10. e
11. g
12. j

Finishing Touches
page 12
1. walk
2. kindle
3. polish
4. whimper
5. harmonize
6. examine
7. comprehend
8. sneeze
9. share
10. exhaust
11. grimace
12. practice
13. crave
14. sparkle
15. heckle
16. tighten

Hide-and-Seek
page 14
1. Bill and Scotty
2. hide-and-seek
3. Answers will vary.
4. he was afraid of the outdoors
5. he was carried to the curb in the garbage can by his brother
6. tears
7. Answers will vary.

Look the Whole World Over
page 15
1. Kyoto, Asia
2. Cairo, Africa
3. Panama City, North America
4. Oslo, Europe
5. Canberra, Australia
6. Saigon, Asia
7. Johannesburg, Africa
8. Eugene, North America

Togetherness
page 16
1. shut
2. stretch
3. Gretel
4. foot
5. Indian
6. dance
7. Odyssey
8. dine
9. goats
10. eggs
11. south
12. Eve
13. roll
14. cheese
15. fall
16. doom
17. winter
18. Q's
19. repel
20. conquer
21. tell
22. Clark
23. fro
24. subtract
25. jelly
26. there
27. saucer

Ripping Jamjams
page 18

1. potent
2. millennium
3. elastic
4. marred
5. savoring
6. thorough
7. beckoned
8. taffy
9. goofy
10. unmercifully
11. martial
12. assorted
13. vied
14. confines
15. shoveled
16. yanked
17. anticipated
18. soared

Hidden Treasures
page 19

1. oil, pan
2. pen, ink
3. ear, lobe
4. oval, round
5. hoot, owl
6. car, auto
7. hair, cut
8. cold, wind
9. show, tell
10. sew, needle
11. mind, matter
12. imp, elf
13. come, go
14. ram, ewe
15. sign, post
16. see, eye
17. sun, ray
18. lad, lass
19. anger, mad
20. ranch, cow
21. love, hate
22. ride, car
23. comb, hair
24. bat, ball

Can It Get Any Better?
page 20

1. bistro
2. mirth
3. exploits
4. investigator
5. flicker
6. turret
7. palpitate
8. detritus
9. horde
10. pretentious
11. demise
12. carafe
13. andante
14. chap
15. umber
16. jade
17. bellowing
18. repel

Rivalry
page 22

Story Title: Rivalry
Characters: Katie, Gwen, Mom
Time: present   Place: Katie's house
Opening Problem: Gwen took Katie's coat
Five main events: Gwen left with Katie's coat
Katie called and left message
Katie waited by the phone
Katie trashed her sister's room
Gwen returned home
Closing Problem: Katie was caught making a mess of Gwen's room
Possible solution: Answers will vary.
Words and meanings: Answers will vary.

Can You Make Heads or Tails out of It?
page 23

1. living high on the hog
2. behind the eight ball
3. down in the mouth
4. pie in the sky
5. bottom line
6. get under your skin
7. wet behind the ears
8. wear your heart on your sleeve
9. pulling your leg

Going for the Gold
page 24

Time Is on Your Side
page 25

Scene 1
4, 2, 7, 1, 5, 3, 6
Scene 2
6, 3, 4, 1, 7, 5, 2
Scene 3
7, 5, 1, 3, 2, 4, 6

Farmer Questions Chicken IQ
page 26

1. Bert Dehaan, Shannon Scratch
2. the farmer claims that his chickens are raising insects for food
3. last Thursday
4. North Dakota
5. Answers will vary.

The Escape
page 28

1. a mystic
2. they can speak to the trees
3. 7
4. at her order trees captured the enemy
5. Answers will vary.
6. pertaining to trees
7. Answers will vary. The were merely servants, her enemies only because of their masters.
8. autumn

I'll File Away
page 29

colors: ebony, amber, crimson, aquamarine
money: lira, peso, yen, rupee
things that light: fire, candle, match, torch
words for praise: applaud, compliment, exalt, laud
trees: fir, acacia, banyan, tamarack
heavy stuff: anvil, rock, elephant, bar bell
things you play: CD, volin, baseball, monopoly
sweets: cookies, honey, pie, candy cane

Are You Conning Me?
page 30

1. congested
2. convince
3. consult
4. contorted
5. converged
6. confabulate
7. conservation
8. contrition
9. conscious
10. conduct
11. conclude
12. controversy
13. conjures
14. contestant
15. confetti
16. concertina
17. content
18. constable

Queen of the Heap
page 32

1. we could sled and ski behind it
2. we had an icy glaze surface on the snow Tuesday
3. I enjoyed living in the country
4. Neddy and Teddy wailed
5. Leanne tried to pull it out

6. it slammed into the manure pile
7. we built a snow fort
8. it tipped over on its side
9. Answers will vary.
10. Answers will vary.

A Moral Dilemma page 34
1. thoughtful, concerned, honest
2. how should he care for the hungry
3. they will continue to beg
   fail to help society
   children forced to beg
4. Answers will vary.
5. Answers will vary.
6. Answers will vary.

It's in Plain English page 35
1. o
2. a
3. j
4. l
5. b
6. f
7. m
8. c
9. n
10. g
11. d
12. k
13. i
14. e
15. h

Like, for Sure! page 36
1. a deaf person could not hear
2. one who is omnipotent is all-powerful
3. if it is vacant, no one is living there
4. one can never reach infinity
5. a silo has no corners
6. ghosts are not living
7. roosters are male—no eggs
8. a small beast cannot tower
9. a carnivore eats meat
10. a void is completely empty
11. bulls are male—no babies
12. pitch-dark means no light—cannot see
13. this tomb contains unidentified soldiers
14. one cannot coast uphill
15. if one is asleep, one cannot verbalize

King of the Mountain! page 38
1. to share a memory of a game called "King of the Mountain"
2. Answers will vary.
3. Double breaker, I'm in Stitches, Almost Disaster, A Hill Thrill
4. a smell discomfort
6. a. lofty—e. very high
   b. pose—f. stance
   c. frenzy—d. madness

You're Never Alone page 39

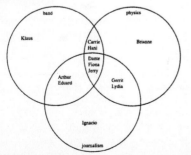

Going to the Hoops page 40
Layne 31
Shane 9
Jane 9
Payne 18
Wayne 34
Zane 17
Tippi 12
Totals, 35, 27, 25, 43, 130

1. Zane
2. 7
3. Payne
4. 1, 4
5. 130
6. 2nd
7. 31
8. Shane, Jane
9. 21
10. 1
11. Payne, Zane
12. 4th

Hello, and Good Evening page 42
1. animal lover
2. meteorologist
3. losing pitcher
4. cobra owner
5. all-state slugger

Report 1 weather
Report 2 deaths
Report 3 sports

Report 1—scorcher, meteorologist, drop
Report 2—tabby, sensitive, donations, lieu
Report 3—thrice, contest, slugfest

I Think I'll Be a . . . . page 43
1. SHIPWRIGHT
2. ARCHITECT
3. DIVER
4. MERCHANT
5. TAILOR
6. MANAGER
7. FARMER
8. ACCOUNTANT
9. SWIMMER
10. DRUMMER
11. PHOTOGRAPHER
12. BUILDER
13. LAWYER
14. DENTIST
15. PILOT
16. METEOROLOGIST
17. BEAUTICIAN
18. EDUCATOR

Trepidation page 44
1. clarinet
2. lips
3. horrendous
4. baton
5. brought
6. awful
7. beet
8. class
9. musical
10. understandingly
11. why
12. Monday
13. smiled
14. squealed
15. lowered
16. band

Smiling page 46
1. 2, 5, 1, 4, 6, 3
2. 4, 2, 1, 6, 3, 5
3. Henry, Mitzi, Shanda, Mother
4. this week
5. Henry's house
6. Henry loses Mitzi
7. Answers will vary.

Got a Match, Bud?   page 47
1. fly   4. vast
2. seas   5. across
3. birds   6. silently
birds silently fly across vast seas
1. climbed   5. creaky
2. obedient   6. pews
3. old   7. children
4. cautiously
cautiously obedient children climbed creaky old pews
1. stout   5. laborers
2. resolutely   6. 144
3. hauled   7. refrigerator
4. cartons
144 stout laborers hauled refrigerator cartons resolutely

Cul-de-sac Heaven   page 48
1. Donnie Jasperse, Pinto, Speedball
2. Erin Ignatius, Quincy, Skateboarding
3. Fabio Kulak, Oakleaf, Street hockey
4. Glen Howard, Nob, Road Croquet

In the Classifieds   page 49
1. h   6. a
2. c   7. d
3. e   8. i
4. j   9. g
5. b   10. f

Plus One   page 50
1. L pelvis   16. A award
2. A chair   17. R winter
3. N never   18. Y year
4. G knight   19. D tried
5. U euchre   20. E spire
6. A urban   21. F flute
7. G rough   22. I indigo
8. E yeast   23. N snag
9. V vital   24. I direct
10. O cough   25. T treat
11. C acorn   26. I naive
12. A pair   27. O moose
13. B superb   28. N round
14. U mules   29. S snow
15. L locust
Language Vocabulary Definitions

Get the Picture   page 51

Inspiration   page 53
1. write a poem
2. no topic came to mind
3. her baby sister
4. holding her in her arms
5. smelly diapers, messy baby food, can't sleep, fussy, burp smells, time with mom

6. keep sister from harm, hold and rock her; Answers will vary.
7. poisonous; toxic
8. to come before, to be more important than
9. clothes, chose
10. ten
11. Answers will vary.
12. Answers will vary.

Here or to Go?   page 54
1. $1.48   4. $9.17
2. Answers will vary. 5. just under 12 hours
3. $3.51   6. $3.04

In the Still of the Night   page 56
1. Keyesha, Bianca, Tonya, Wanda
   state forest
   a summer night
   Wanda missing; "blood" found
2. 2, 5, 3, 4, 6, 1
3. Answers will vary.
4. Answers will vary.

I've Got a Secret   page 57
1. bat   7. rabbit
2. spider   8. ant
3. duck   9. hummingbird
4. moths   10. monarch butterfly
5. frog   11. blue racer
6. opossum   12. pike

Guilt   page 59
1. he broke his Mama's dish
2. his tears
3. a. not to draw attention
   b. to hold the pain inside
4. Answers will vary.
5. Answers will vary.
6. Answers will vary.
7. a. missive b. comforter c. plunked

Food for Thought   page 60
Spices: cinnamon, cloves, cumin, curry, ginger, nutmeg, paprika, pepper
Desserts: apple dumpling, cobbler, eclair, fudge, pumpkin pie, sorbet, strudel, truffle
Drinks: cider, cola, eggnog, hot cocoa, juice, malt, milk, wassail
Grains/Breads: bagel, barley, cereal, cracker, oatmeal, pasta, rice, tortilla

Memorials   page 61
1. battle   2. tongues
   attle   ctongues
   apple   ctonseug
   appel   ctrnseug
   appeal   ctrpseug
   aealpp   actrapseug
   elpp   actrpaseug
   pplre   craeg
   pluntplre   robraep
   mountmore   pearbor
   Mount Rushmore   Pearl Harbor

With the Guys
page 63
1. Answers will vary.
2. the gang hangs together but leaves out Junior
3. the gang forces Junior to leave
4. this gang attitude toward Junior seems to be a bad idea
5. Mike—thoughtful   Nick—bully
   gang—followers   June—isolated
6. Answers will vary.
7. feel comfortable with each other; trust; unity
8. when it causes a group to isolate others, ignore compassion, become blind to the greater community

Commonality
page 64
2. Edison, Carver
3. damask, linen
4. label, novel
5. Denver, Amman
6. bottle, basket
7. rotund, spherical
8. north, above
9. balloon, tuba
10. piano, forte
11. Bo Peep, Jill
12. reggae, jazz
13. linebacker, receiver
14. rubella, strep throat
15. fuchsia, amber
16. Lincoln Memorial, Capitol
17. postcard, novelty mug
18. Sphinx, minaret
19. Caspian Sea, Missouri River
20. Ella Fitzgerald, Buddy Holly
21. Lady Macbeth, Ophelia
22. satellite, telegraph
23. Colombia, Bolivia
24. glide, soar

Proverbial Wisdom
page 65
1. dessert
2. wise
3. hands
4. together
5. germ
6. keeps
7. lanes
8. ready
9. calm
10. musician
11. parted
12. begging
13. floated
14. lake
15. chasm
16. look

The Hands of Rodin
page 67
I. B. Rounded wings (comic, playful)
   C. Tunic of metal disks
II. *The Supper Table*
   A. Low thick-legged table
   C. Knives and forks glazed in silver
   E. Wood-like candle stick with wax candle
III. A. Cityscape of towers, spires, many geometric shapes
   B. Ribbon-like highways pull city together
   D. A center of green—a central park
   medium—paper

The Writers' Block
page 68
1. d
2. i
3. g
4. a
5. c
6. f
7. h
8. b
9. e
10. n
11. l
12. q
13. j
14. k
15. p
16. r
17. m
18. o
19. u
20. y
21. w
22. s
23. v
24. z
25. x
26. t

What's the Word?
page 69
1. kiosk
2. examined
3. fidgeting
4. brink
5. opinion
6. grateful
7. trust
8. innkeeper
9. loft
10. unicorn
11. core
12. nonsense
13. drape
14. endear
15. vital
16. slumber
17. urchin
18. quartet
19. yearned
20. habituate

Write Me a Letter
page 71
1. Hawaii
2. less than 2 months
3. summer exchange student
4. girl
5. probably 16-17
6. Biology
7. exotic bird—parrot
8. Japan
9. Toronto, Ontario
10. soccer

Lay It on the Line
page 72
in a nutshell
can't hold a candle to
all ears
cool it
too big for her britches
sitting duck
fly the coop
hit the nail on the head
one-track mind
over a barrel
cat got your tongue
out of the clear blue sky

A Far-Off Place
page 73
1. Em
2. Hal, Garth
3. snow
4. Bob and Em
5. Chloe, Dot, and Em
6. 10 cm
7. only month with more hail than snow
8. 75 cm
9. 62 cm
10. a. Dot   f. Fern
    b. Chloe   g. Irma
    c. Em   h. Garth
    d. Bob   i. Hal
    e. Alf

Peppermints
page 75
1. youth, painfully patient, motion
2. Da wants to sit in a certain pew in church
3. candy shepherd; the children flock around him
4. a. Da couldn't find keys   b. Marty needed hair braided
   c. Hannah lost her shoes
5. the peppermint is stuck in her throat
6. she spits it up
7. Answers will vary.
8. Answers will vary.

Fly This Past Me
page 76
1. ospry
2. swallow
3. pelican
4. bluejay
5. chickadee
6. oriole
7. cardinal
8. cormorant
9. parakeet
10. peacock

Take Your Pic
page 77

1. d
2. f
3. g
4. b
5. h
6. e
7. a
8. c

Telling Tales
page 79

1. Goldilocks and the Three Bears
2. Papa Bear
3. Answers will vary.
4. A few possibilities are: "Did you get a good look at the intruder?" "How did she get into your house?" "How do you know she had toast?" "Did the intruder enter other rooms?"
5. Answer will vary.
6. Mama Bear was stung by a bee—allergic reaction
7. audacity—arrogance, nerve
   varmint—troublesome creature
8. psychologically damaged

In the Mood
page 80

1. e
2. a
3. c
4. d
5. b
6. b
7. d
8. e
9. a
10. c
11. e
12. c
13. d
14. a
15. b

Mm-Mm-Good!
page 81

1. macaque
2. mackintosh
3. madcap
4. magenta
5. magnify
6. maize
7. malicious
8. mamba
9. manor
10. maraca
11. marten
12. matador
13. mattock
14. matrimony
15. matzo
16. meager
17. mayhap
18. meander
19. measles
20. melodious
21. memento
22. meteor
23. mew
24. mingle

American Graffiti
page 83

1. television
2. spunk
3. Answers will vary.
4. Answers will vary.
5. Answers will vary.
6. Answers will vary.
7. Answers will vary.

Black, White, and Read All Over
page 84

1. g
2. d
3. b
4. c
5. a
6. h
7. e
8. f

Somewhere Out There
page 86

It's True!
page 88

1. Ole Bergstrom
2. Old World, Michigan
3. 1860-1880s
4. Answers will vary. Some possibilities are loading coal, clearing land, fighting fire.
5. a. mum—l. quiet
   b. merchant—g. trader
   c. hoosegow—h. jail
   d. privy—k. rustic bathroom
   e. peavey—j. loggers pole
   f. shanty boy—i. lumberjack

Moving Right Along
page 89

Oops! Sorry!
page 90

Andrew, Hanna, Pop
Bao, Iola, pretzels
Charlie, Gigi, cookies
Don, Fern, chips
Emilio, Jasmine, carrots/celery

Fee, Fi!
page 92

1. 5   2
   7   1
   4   6
   3
2. a. outcast, lonely
   b. perseverence
   c. comfort, empathy
   d. indignation
3. Answers will vary.

Data Doubled
page 93

1. 54
2. 29
3. 57
4. boys
5. 113
6. Room B
7. Room A
8. Room D
9. communications
10. 11 students

In Your Face   **page 94**

With You   **page 96**
1. raises apples on a farm
2. the bowling alley
3. to be with his papa, answers will vary
4. bubblegum will pop in his face
5. Papa might be very angry. The gum was a present.
6. Answers will vary.

A Contractual Agreement   **page 97**
1. 4 weeks
2. 1968 Lolich Lane
3. 6
4. president of Sports Freaks
5. no
6. so lawn service can do its work
7. $1,200
8. Perry Winkle
9. 24 (or 25) weeks
10. Monday or Tuesday
Extra: Answers will vary.

Students in Sports   **page 98**
1. soccer, cycling, cross-country
2. January-March
3. girls
4. boys
5. December, April
6. February/March
7. 137
8. 66.5
9. 64.5

How'd You Like That?   **page 100**
1. Native Americans of the Great Plains
2. bison
3. poor weapons
4. skins of animals
5. hunters
6. horse made travel easier; better weapons—rifle
7. boisterous, thunderous
8. grooves
9. scent

What's the Word?   **page 101**
1. stupid   6. hat
2. monotony   7. unwatchful
3. potato   8. muscular strength
4. Inuit boat   9. glass bottle
5. bad reputation   10. pause
mystery word: jubilation

Pop Out   **page 103**
1. quickly
   dangerously
   yell loudly
   small enclosure
   anything you could imagine
   transport
   high-pitched little kids
   sped
   metal bolt
   villanious
   open wide
2. Answers will vary.
3. Answers will vary.

Sanitation Engineer   **page 104**
1. tail   9. Realizing
2. mess   10. table
3. myself   11. tackle
4. Saturday   12. lying
5. loudly   13. cereal
6. grouchy   14. wrappers
7. doing   15. gloated
8. down   16. mouth

Drive Like Jehu   **page 106**
1. rural area, allows for speed and bus stop
2. timely
3. a chariot driver mentioned in the Bible
4. crevise, abyss, cavity
5. drainpipe
6. "Dad is a crazy driver" becomes "Dad as a sensation"
7. drives vehicle very fast

Top Secret   **page 107**
1. injure   7. whirlwinds
2. cumbersome   8. hygiene
3. concrete   9. bacteria
4. deadlock   10. nocturnal
5. wrangle   11. excessive
6. reference   12. security

Hit or Myth   **page 108**
1. Pan   13. centaur
2. Poseidon   14. hydra
3. Prometheus   15. Hera
4. Uranus   16. Atalanta
5. Artemis   17. Hermes
6. Helios   18. Aphrodite
7. Hades   19. Orion
8. Demeter   20. Minotaur
9. Cyclops   21. Heracles
10. Atlas   22. Ares
11. Zeus   23. Gaea
12. Apollo   24. Athena

Stormy Weather   **page 110**
1. 7, 3, 6, 2, 5, 1, 4
2. clouds-charcoal gray   whispering stir of wind
   rumble of thunder   lightning slashed
3. Answers will vary.

Haste Makes Waste page 111

1. June
2. Movers
3. appreciate
4. Steinway
5. slogan
6. complaints
7. finely
8. gouged
9. entrance
10. neighboring
11. slid
12. in
13. repair
14. Cost
15. cosmetic
16. haste
17. apparently
18. inside
19. civilly
20. contact

London's Calling page 112

1. clarinet
2. Hansel
3. plover
4. align
5. bone
6. follow
7. football
8. fifth
9. Macbeth
10. bowl
11. Lisbon
12. island
13. squid

The Call of the Wild
Jack London

The Visit page 114

1. Costa Rica
2. America
3. She didn't trust the country's food.
4. felt like everyone was watching
5. going to another country; seeing Abbie again
6. Answers will vary.
7. Answers will vary.
8. Answers will vary.
9. Answers will vary.
10. Answers will vary.

Three Cases page 115

1.

	fraction	$	-$4	+½$	new total
first	½	30	26	+13	$39.00
second	⅗₀	18	14	+7	$21.00
third	⅖	12	8	+4	$12.00

2. cedar spruce larch hemlock pine
3. Robby—grandfather
   Bob—mother
   Rob—son

She's in the Money page 116

1. $2638
2. $2766
3. $128

	Value	Gain
8:00	$2638	-0-
8:30	2646	8
9:00	2654	16
9:30	2662	24
10:00	2670	32
10:30	2678	40
11:00	2686	48
11:30	2694	56
12:00	2702	64
12:30	2710	72
1:00	2718	80
1:30	2726	88
2:00	2734	96
2:30	2742	104
3:00	2750	112
3:30	2758	120
4:00	2766	128